THE
9 DECLARATIONS

I.   MEET LIFE WITH FULL PRESENCE AND POWER

II.   RECLAIM YOUR AGENDA

III. DEFEAT YOUR DEMONS

IV.   ADVANCE WITH ABANDON

V.   PRACTICE JOY AND GRATITUDE

VI.   DO NOT BREAK INTEGRITY

VII. AMPLIFY LOVE

VIII. INSPIRE GREATNESS

IX.   SLOW TIME

THE
MOTIVATION
MANIFESTO

9 Declarations to Claim
Your Personal Power

BRENDON BURCHARD

HAY HOUSE, INC.

Carlsbad, California • New York City

London • Sydney • Johannesburg

Vancouver • Hong Kong • New Delhi

Published and distributed in the United States by: Hay House, Inc.: www.hayhouse.com® • Published and distributed in Australia by: Hay House Australia Pty. Ltd.: www.hayhouse.com.au • Published and distributed in the United Kingdom by: Hay House UK, Ltd.: www.hayhouse.co.uk • Published and distributed in the Republic of South Africa by: Hay House SA (Pty), Ltd.: www.hayhouse.co.za • Distributed in Canada by: Raincoast Books: www.raincoast.com • Published in India by: Hay House Publishers India: www.hayhouse.co.in

Cover design: Brendon Burchard
Interior design: Charles McStravick
Author illustration: Nancy Januzzi

Cataloging-in-Publication Data is on file at the Library of Congress

Hardcover ISBN: 978-1-4019-4807-8

10 9 8 7 6 5 4 3 2 1
1st edition, October 2014

SUSTAINABLE FORESTRY INITIATIVE
Certified Chain of Custody
Promoting Sustainable Forestry
www.sfiprogram.org
SFI-01268
SFI label applies to the text stock

PRINTED IN THE UNITED STATES OF AMERICA

CONTENTS

All religions, arts and sciences are branches of the same tree.
All these aspirations are directed toward ennobling man's life,
lifting it from the sphere of mere physical existence
and leading the individual towards freedom.

ALBERT EINSTEIN

Conformity is the jailer of freedom
and the enemy of growth.

JOHN F. KENNEDY

THE DECLARATION OF
PERSONAL POWER

THERE COMES A TIME IN THE LIVES OF THOSE DESTINED for greatness when we must stand before the mirror of meaning and ask: *Why, having been endowed with the courageous heart of a lion, do we live as mice?*

We must look squarely into our own tired eyes and examine why we waste so much time sniffing at every distraction, why we cower at the thought of revealing our true selves to the world, why we scurry so quickly from conflict, and why we consent to play small. We must ask why we participate so humbly in society's frantic race, allowing ourselves into its mazes of mediocrity and settling for scraps of reward when nature has offered unlimited freedom, power, and abundance to the bold, the determined, the creative, the independent—to *each of us*. We must ask if our desires to feel safe and accepted are in fact enslaving us to popular opinion—and to boredom. We must ask: *When will we be ready to ascend to another level of existence?*

When in the course of human events it becomes necessary to ask such questions and to dissolve the beliefs and behaviors that have limited us, assuming once more the full powers of our being to which God and the laws of nature have entitled us, a decent respect to humankind requires that we should declare the motives that impel us to exert our strength and to separate ourselves from those who stunt our vitality, growth, and happiness.

We must declare our personal power and freedom.

We hold these truths self-evident: That all men and women are created equal, though we do not live equal lives due to differences in will, motivation, effort, and habit. That we are endowed by our Creator with certain inalienable Rights, that among these are Life, Liberty, and the pursuit of Happiness, but that it is incumbent upon each of us to be vigilant and disciplined should we wish to attain such a vital, free, and happy life. We believe the greatest of human powers is the ability to independently think for ourselves, to choose our own aims, affections, and actions. For in the hearts of humankind lives a natural instinct for freedom and independence, a psychological predisposition for self-direction, a biological imperative toward growth, and a spiritual joy in choosing and advancing one's own life. It is the main motivation of humankind to be free, to express our true selves and pursue our dreams without restriction—to experience what may be called Personal Freedom.

To secure these Rights and this Personal Freedom, men and women of conscience must not consent to be controlled by fear, convention, or the will of the masses. We must govern our own lives, and when our thoughts and actions become destructive it is our responsibility to alter or abolish them and to institute new habits as the foundations for a freer, happier life. We must exert our power, improving how we think and how we interact with the world.

When a long chain of self-oppressions and social controls has reduced our strength and independence, it is our right—our *duty*—to throw off such a life, rise anew, and charge unencumbered through the gates of greatness.

We have patiently suffered long enough, hoping that someone or some kind of luck would one day grant us more opportunity and happiness. But nothing external can save us, and the fateful hour is at hand when we either become trapped at this level of life or we choose to ascend to a higher plane of consciousness and joy. In this ailing and turbulent world, we must find peace within and become more self-reliant in creating the life we deserve.

This will be a difficult effort, as the history of our actions too often tells a tale of self-injury and unhappiness, stemming from our blind desire to be judged worthy, acceptable, and lovable by people who hardly know our true hearts and powers. And so we have kept ourselves down: We forgot to set clear intentions and standards, and too often failed to voice our desires and dreams. Randomness and mediocrity too often ruled the day, and the loud and the needy dictated who we were and what we should do—our lives becoming subject to the tyranny of fools. If we can be vulnerable and brave enough to admit such missteps, we might see the potential we left unrealized; we might see a shining new path.

And so let us right our lives. Let us face the mirror and be candid. No matter what we see, let us use these common human truths and personal declarations to reclaim our freedom:

We are too often lost in the abyss of unawareness. We regularly miss the energy and blessings around us, and the importance of this very moment. It's as though we prefer to be elsewhere doing something else, as if we are living in distant time zones, hours behind or ahead of the joyous tick and bliss of Now. We have forgotten that the natural foe to life is not a distant death, but a present, in-the-moment detachment from living. Should we wish to be free and alive with full power, we must decide to bring the full might of our conscious mind to the present experience. We must choose to *feel* again. We must set intentions for who we are, for what roles we wish to serve, for how we'll relate with the world. Without a vibrant awareness, we cannot connect with others or ourselves, nor can we meet the demands of the hour with grace. For this, we now declare: **WE SHALL MEET LIFE WITH FULL PRESENCE AND POWER.**

We have ceded control of our daily lives. Amid incessant distraction, our discipline in pursuing high ambitions has vanished. The white space of a free day seems unfathomable because we have become hypnotized by a false but compelling need to respond to all the needs of others. We are pulled at from every angle, torn from meaningful efforts by frivolous pursuits or false emergencies, and we are often unsure how to balance our lives with the needs of those we love. We are too often detached from what is most worth fighting for; our busywork consumes our day but it is not our life's work. Most do not feel a stark, stirring life purpose—they don't hunger for it in the morning or orient their day to its pursuit. A life of greater joy, power, and satisfaction awaits those who consciously design their life. For this, we now declare: WE SHALL RECLAIM OUR AGENDA.

Something inside is sabotaging our natural drive toward freedom. It whines and roars for us to stop whenever we push beyond our comforts; whenever we choose to be authentic and loving in a scary world; whenever we seek to make a difference at the cost of our own position; whenever we desire something magnificent that, to obtain, would require hardship and work. Our internal demons poison us with worry and fear whenever we might be vulnerable, stunting our growth and vitality. Our destiny is decided by how well we know our demons of Doubt and Delay, how well we defend against them, and how many battles we win against them each day of our lives. Without self-mastery, we are slaves to fear. With it, greatness and transcendence are ours. For this, we now declare: WE SHALL DEFEAT OUR DEMONS.

Most of us are not maturing as fast as we are able. We are on constant pause; we wait and we wait, to find out who we are, to declare our dreams, to struggle for what we want, to open ourselves fully to love and to life. We await personal courage to arise within us, or for society to grant us some ill-defined permission to activate our potential. We have forgotten that courage is a choice, and that permission to move forward with boldness is never given by the fearful masses. Most have forgotten that seeking change always requires a touch of insanity. If taking action before the perfect conditions arise, or before we receive permission, is unreasonable or reckless, then we must be unreasonable and reckless. We must remember we are not the sum of our intentions but of our actions. Bold and disciplined initiative is our savior; it allows us to rise, to leap, to soar to the heights of true greatness. We must not lose the urgency of this moment as it begs for us to begin something grand and important. For this, we now declare: **WE SHALL ADVANCE WITH ABANDON.**

We are exhausted. All around us we see faces that look weathered, drooped, stern. We hear conversations that sound increasingly quiet and resigned, like whispers from a tired, disbanding tribe. The emotional energy of the world is flatlining. Well-being has been cast aside for wealth; success favored over sanity. In the process, some have turned cold toward life, and toward others. Where is the energized, heightened, exhilarated pulse one would expect from such a chosen and capable people? Why do we not hear more laughter and life? Where is the vibrant, mad fury and passion of the fully engaged human? Where are the people burning with charisma and joy and magnetism? Where is the appreciation for life's spark? We must reexamine our attitude toward life. Our supreme duty must be to rekindle the magic of life. For this, we now declare: **WE SHALL PRACTICE JOY AND GRATITUDE.**

We compromise too easily when life becomes difficult. Most sacrifice individuality and integrity without a fight, although arrogance prevents seeing this truth. Too many of us believe ourselves strong when a long gaze across our lives would sight a pattern of quitting or withdrawing too soon, often when our loved ones needed us to be strong or right when our dreams were just within reach. For convenience or the wide smile of popularity, we waffle on our word and give up what we truly believe in. But there is a nobility to those who do not let neediness or desperation compromise who they are. We must not follow any impulse to be weak or heartless. Instead we must have a strong refusal to break, choosing that mighty lift of courage, that soaring commitment to love, that grand ascent to the realm of character that is congruent with our highest values. Freedom and victory belong to those who remain true and strong despite temptation. For this, we now declare: **WE SHALL NOT BREAK OUR INTEGRITY.**

We are not transmitting or receiving love as we were divinely intended to—we are filtering love rather than feeling it. We fell for the prevailing hysteria that said, "Protect your heart," and we began to believe that love itself had enemies and needed protecting. When we were hurt, we felt that love was somehow diminished or damaged. But hurt has nothing to do with love, and love is unaffiliated with and unaffected by pain. Ego was hurt, not love. Love is divine; it is everywhere, ever present and abundant and free. It is a spiritual energy that is, at this very moment, flowing through the universe—through us, through our enemies, through our families, through billions of souls. It was never absent from our lives. It is not bound in our hearts or in our relationships, and thus it is not capable of being owned or lost. We have allowed our awareness of love to diminish; that is all. In doing so, we have caused our own suffering. We must mature and realize that freeing our mind of ancient hurts and opening once more to love shall give us access to divine strength. To stand emotionally open before the world and give of our hearts without fear of hurt or demand of reciprocity—this is the ultimate act of human courage. For this, we now declare: WE SHALL AMPLIFY LOVE.

Generation after generation is failing to hold the line on the ideals and virtues of humanity. The low hum of mediocrity and the heinous pitch of narcissism have replaced what was once the chorus of society singing to virtue, progress, and selflessness. Our talents and collective focus are not fully invested in personal mastery and social contribution but squandered on voyeurism and base sensationalism. Too often we don't call out a wrong or expect ourselves or others to act with routine integrity, excellence, or love. There has been a worldwide failure in leadership, birthing an apathetic populace, unjustifiable poverty, unconscionable greed, and a globe ravaged and booby-trapped by war. So many people are afraid to demand more—to dare, as have the great leaders of the past, to incite the directionless with bold challenges to rise and contribute. *We* must do better. From the squalor of a contaminated moral environment must surface an honorable few, unafraid to challenge the direction of the world. History shall fill in the wake of our actions, so let us be purposeful and let us be great. For this, we now declare: WE SHALL INSPIRE GREATNESS.

Hurry has become the master. We have stopped sensing the stillness, the stunning fullness and beauty and divine perfection of the moment. Most barrel through life, unaware of their senses and surroundings, deaf and blind to the magical qualities of . . . *this* . . . *very* . . . *moment.* We are not supposed to miss it all, this *life,* but we do, all frazzled, stressed, and stripped away from Now. The cost is immense—so many moments blurred by speed and worry and panic, all stacking onto hectic days, all creating the catastrophe of an un-experienced, joyless life. Many can only vaguely remember the last time they laughed so hard it hurt, loved so much it led to a beautiful flood, cheered so loudly it strained the vocal chords, felt so deeply it caused a showering of tears, had such a raucously good time that it became legend—moments fully *lived.* We must s – l – o – w it all down, not just to become more present in the singular moment, but also to elongate that moment so that we truly *sense* it. Life is meant to be a vibrant, deeply felt, growing mosaic of long, meaningful moments. This day is to be enjoyed like a pause at a cool stream during summer's heat. For this, we now declare: WE SHALL SLOW TIME.

Most of these problems in our lives have been self-imposed. Yet even when we became conscious of them, we sought change in the most humble terms: we set realistic goals and worked to achieve them. But fearful of unleashing our full power, we saw our will fade, we aimed low, and even our mighty efforts were dampened by distraction or the criticisms of a conformist culture. We complained with angst and anger that it should be easier, forgetting that much of the negative energy that pervades our lives comes from despising the inevitable hardships of change.

Let us remember that humanity's story has only two perennially recurring themes: *struggle* and *progress*. We mustn't wish the end of the former, as the latter would be buried alongside it. And so let us be clear that the small, complaining, undisciplined part of ourselves—the distracted character wanting nothing but convenience and ease—is unfit to be the ruler of our new destiny.

Nor can we allow apathetic, small-thinking men and women to lay waste to our future. We mustn't let social pressures poison our potential. Surely, we have warned others from time to time that we do not care what they think or that their judgments of us are unwarranted. We have often complained, made kind requests of others, or reminded people of the circumstances that made us want to improve our lives. We have appealed to their magnanimity to be gentler or more supportive, and we have asked them as kindred spirits to stand with us against those who interrupt our charge. Yet too often others have been deaf to our true voices. They didn't believe in us or support us or cheer us on when it mattered most. We must, therefore, not await their assistance or approval any longer. We must hold them, as we hold the rest of mankind, enemies in battle should they stand in the way of our dreams, but in peace and assistance, friends.

Let us awaken now and realize there is greater vibrancy, joy, and freedom available to each of us. There is more feeling. There is more power. There is more love and abundance. But gaining access rests on our shoulders, for only two things can change our lives: either something new comes into our lives, or something new comes *from within*. Let us not hope for mere chance to change our story; let us summon the courage to change it ourselves. Some will stand in our way, but we mustn't hide or minimize ourselves any longer. Let us believe faithfully that our dreams are worth any struggle and that it is our time to free ourselves and rise to glory.

WE THEREFORE, as free women and men of courage and conscience, appealing to our Creator for the strength to live our intentions, do, in the name of our Destiny, solemnly publish and declare that our lives are—and, of right, ought to be—free and independent. We declare that we are absolved from allegiance to those who oppress or hurt us, and that all social connections between us and them are and ought to be totally dissolved, and that as free and independent persons, we have the full power to exert our true strength, live our dreams, find peace, create wealth, love openly those who have our hearts, contribute without fear or permission, strive for personal greatness, serve the common good, and do all other acts and things that independent and motivated persons have the right to do. And for the support of this Declaration, with a firm reliance on the protection of divine Providence, we pledge our Lives, our Fortunes, and our sacred Honor.

ON HUMAN NATURE

———

FREEDOM, FEAR, AND MOTIVATION

I

ON FREEDOM

I want freedom for the full expression of my personality.

MAHATMA GANDHI

A VIBRANT, GENUINE, AND PURPOSEFUL LIFE IS THE right of all humankind. But most of us fail to grasp it. We are lions and lionesses living as mice. Rather than exploring free on the savanna, we are living small and distracted lives. It is the calling of each man and woman who draws breath to have a grand vision for our lives, and to, each day, claim the vastness of that vision. Yet rather than stalk our dreams with abandon, we too often sit and sulk, blaming and complaining, chasing after paltry goals that cheat the magnificence of our being. Is this our true nature?

Surely not. We are all meant to be wild and independent and free, our hearts filled with a ferocious passion for life. The day is meant to be ours, and our purpose within it is to live as who we truly are and enjoy the full terrain of life's freedom as we chase our own meaning and purpose, our own legacy. If we can unchain ourselves from social restrictions, we can have that day, and we can leap and stretch, expressing our power to its limits. We can hunt our dreams with a fierceness unimagined by those creatures trapped in wastelands of stress and sorrow.

So let us not forget the thing we are after:

Humankind's main motivation is to seek and experience Personal Freedom.

This is neither a political statement nor necessarily a Western philosophy. It would be difficult to deny that all people worldwide deeply desire the grand freedoms—social freedom, emotional freedom, creative freedom, financial freedom, time freedom, and spiritual freedom. No matter a person's religion or spiritual or life philosophy, they want the freedom to exercise it. This argument carries on: no matter how someone wants to feel in life, they want the freedom to feel it; no matter what one wants to create and contribute, they want freedom to do so; no matter what someone dreams of doing with their work time or free time, they want the freedom to direct it and enjoy it; no matter one's political perspective, they want the freedom to follow it and support it. And so at the base of all of our desires is the greater desire for freedom to *choose* and *actualize* that desire.

Choosing our own aims and seeking to bring them to fruition creates a sense of vitality and motivation in life. The only things that derail our efforts are fear and oppression.

That is ultimately what Personal Freedom is: liberty from the restrictions of *social* oppression and the tragic *self-*oppression that is *fear.* Freed from these things, we have the ability to express who we truly are and pursue what we deeply desire without restrictions set by others or ourselves.

When experiencing Personal Freedom, we have a heightened sense of *genuineness* and *joy* in our being. We feel unbounded, independent, and self-reliant. There is a palpable authenticity and aliveness in how we relate to others and contribute to the world.

Personal Freedom—our goal—means:

- living freely by crafting a life on our own terms;

- being free in the moment from oppressions, of past hurts and present anxieties;

- being lighthearted and spontaneous as free spirits;

- courageously speaking our thoughts, feelings, and ambitions with those around us, without concern about acceptance;

- enjoying our free will to pursue abundant happiness, wealth, health, achievement, and contribution;

- freely loving whom we choose with passionate abandon;

- standing freely on our own, professing and protecting our ideas and integrity;

- serving a mission that we have chosen;

- fighting to give our children a foundation in such freedom, building in their hearts the will to live as they choose so that they may meet oppression with courage, and opportunity with a virtuous intent to contribute.

Can anyone deny that these are things all humans desire and strive for?

The call for individual freedom as the great human drive has been expressed for centuries by revolutionists, humanitarians, philosophers, and spiritual leaders. We have heard its essence voiced as the *inalienable right of humankind* to think for ourselves, to speak our minds, pursue happiness, seek peace and prosperity, and sing to our own conception of the Divine without the conformity imposed by small minds or our own small-mindedness.

Outside of tyrants oppressing their people through fear, this common argument is made across most modern cultures, political movements, and areas of human study: *each of us, every individual, ought to have the right to happily and peacefully move our lives forward without fear or hurt or imprisonment or arbitrary social constraints.*

We inherently know that, when controlled by others, life loses its flair and we are cast into melancholy and mediocrity. Without such striving for individual freedom, what becomes of us? We relinquish our free will to a society of strangers that speaks not of liberty and courage but of conformity and caution. Our true self is subjugated and a pseudo self emerges, a mere reflection of a society that has lost its way. "They" start running our lives and soon we are not "us" anymore, just walking zombies filled with the commands of others' preferences and expectations. We become those masked souls who spend their time wandering in a wildernesses of sameness and sadness. We become tired and weak. We lose our nature. And then we see the worst of human behavior—a mass of people who do not speak up for themselves or others but rather do only what they are told.

From this reality the worst of human horrors emerged in our past: the mass murders of races and classes because the powerful elite or the churches said to scorch the earth or cleanse the souls, the Holocaust cast upon millions as the world looked on for too long before acting, the mass indifference of a society that allows its people to starve and struggle, the despicable acts of mobs and madmen who simply do not respect the freedom or rights of the individual human. When freedom is gone, suffering sets in for all.

Why does freedom pull so tightly at our hearts?

It is because freedom is tightly bound to the human desire for *ascension*—our natural drive to rise from our circumstances and actualize our goals, our potential, our highest self.

All things that make life worthwhile to great men and women—the pursuit of happiness, challenge, progress, creative expression, contribution, hard-won wisdom, and enlightenment—derive from our *wanting to ascend to higher levels of being and giving.*

Every human has a natural inclination to ascend to higher planes of existence, but it rests upon each of us to match that inclination with real initiative. We must remember that freedom can be achieved only by diligent will and volition. Seeking to ascend in life takes grit and resolve, struggle and courage. But to those who make the effort belong all the glories of life and history. Consider that the great masters and leaders of yesterday trained themselves to be free from social and self-oppressions to an impressive degree. They struggled but learned to be free in the moment to express who they truly were and to create and contribute to the world without paralyzing fear. They didn't feel the need to conform but rather learned to be independent, unique, and genuine, even as they successfully served the world, even as they were often judged or jailed. On the ground of such personal liberation stand the world's most noble figures: Gandhi and Frankl and King and Mandela were free even as they were imprisoned.

Just look back at history, and freedom leaps from the page as iconic metaphors:

It's the brave revolutionist, who we saw as the lonely figure on the scaffold, refusing to recant his beliefs and quit the fight for independence.

It's every great revolt we celebrate, when we saw the outnumbered take the field against bigger, better-armed forces, ready to be massacred so that their children may stand a fighting chance at seeing freedom another day.

It's the forming of new nations, where we saw bombs bursting in air and the homes of the brave being built on the foundation of liberty.

It's the race for new lands, where we saw wild horses thundering westward, carrying even wilder men racing to stake their claim for a new life.

It's the soul of the Civil War, where we saw neighbors divided into blue and gray, killing one another, bloodying the earth of their homeland, and yet rising eventually as one to abolish the idea that their fellow humans should ever be enslaved.

It's the breaking of earthly bonds, where we saw two brothers on a homemade flyer slip the surly bonds of gravity.

It's the drive behind the First World War, where we saw mud- and bloodstained faces thousands of miles from home, dressed in olive drab, armed with nothing but knives and rifles and canteens and senses of duty, honor, and country.

It's the fight against Hitler, where we saw that tiny, evil tyrant—monstrously enraged, inflicting horror and death on millions—finally destroyed by a band of nations, one led by a free man in a wheelchair.

It's the greatest dream ever voiced, where we saw thousands march in fearful, bigoted towns against a wave of pick handles and dogs and fire hoses; where we saw hundreds of thousands march to that shining city on a hill, to listen to one man's dream to let freedom ring.

It's that giant leap of mankind, where we saw that small metal capsule carry brave men in white, puffy suits beyond the blue sky into the blackness, transcending their own earthly limits, landing on the moon, coming home to a world that could never again believe in the impossible.

It's the crumbling of the Berlin Wall, where we saw millions hungering for freedom tearing down the real and metaphorical wall dividing humanity. Decades and thousands of miles away, in another country whose great wall still stands, we saw a little man in a large public square stand defiantly in front of an oncoming tank, proclaiming his right to freedom.

These are the enduring images of our history, colored by the blood, tears, toil, and sweat of those who sought and fought for some form of liberation. Over and over, we see millions march, millions fight, millions die, and millions thrive, all in the cause of freedom.

The ultimate narrative of the human species
is its quest for more freedom
and the related struggles to ascend
to higher standards of living and relating.

In such divine desires to overcome tyranny, oppression, and the limits of our own darkness and small-mindedness, we find recurrent hope for humanity.

Those who found hope and lived a free and happy life despite history's brutalities and darkness were not simply people of fortune or luck or fame, but rather of conscience and courage. They knew the demands of their time, that their destiny was unfolding with the man or woman to their left and to their right, and that they would need to remain motivated in overcoming both their internal demons and the social tyrants of the world. Theirs was a long march of effort and endurance and enlightenment. They declared without apologies their independence, their rights and direction. Their only guide was an internal one, a manifesto in their minds that called for the courage to be themselves and the discipline to direct their energies toward higher purposes.

Because of their example, we have many social freedoms to be thankful for. Worldwide, political freedom continues to grow or be desired. Financial freedoms are beginning to extend to more corners of the globe. Individuality and uniqueness is winning in commerce. All the freedoms we take for granted in the more liberated and abundant cultures—

convenience on every corner, safety from physical threat, wide access to education and health care—arrived on the backs of men and women dedicated to some form of freedom.

For this, we owe previous generations—and, in respect, future generations—no less than to seek and find our own modern Personal Freedom. For this, we must awake each day in utter clarity that these are deeply momentous hours in our lives, when we will either shrink from similar greatness, preferring the approval of small minds, or stand on the shoulders of the noble and free people who refused to settle. So let us each in our own way and in our own voice echo their courage and proclaim freedom as our fight, our cause, the very challenge we awaken to experience and achieve.

THE DOUBTS ABOUT FREEDOM

Some have questioned if we have too much freedom, if our great liberties are too much of a good thing. The long light of this golden age of peace and prosperity has changed the world for the better, but for some, it has led to a sunburn on the soul—an excessive exposure to abundance that has led to indolence, greed, narcissism, and entitlement.

But such people, even as they might live in the more politically liberated patches of Earth, are not in truth free. They are caged by their own recurring vices. The man afflicted by hunger for power or money for its own sake is just that: afflicted. He is tormented by incessant desires for more without cause. He is the most likely to wear a social mask to succeed, and thus he is always unsure of himself and his life, the deep tear inside always causing him to obsess about how to get more, why he doesn't have it already, and whom he will have to please or become in order to get it. The woman afflicted by the need for adoration cannot have a free moment of real joy away from her obsession with self; she is slave to the never-ending quest for youth and beauty and social acceptance. Her endless desire blinds her from areas for growth and alienates others, ripping away her chances at genuine self-expression and the soaring kind of true love she deserves. And for the entitled, there can be only a constant whining misery; no person who believes they should be given everything for nothing will ever be free from an immature envy and contempt for those who have more than they do. The entitled are perhaps the most caged of all, slave to a grand fiction that the world owes them anything at all.

So we find that even in abundant and politically "free" cultures there is still the tyranny of conformity coupled with inner turmoil.

This brings us back once again to the focus on Personal Freedom. The cause does not disappear simply because there is political or financial freedom.

There will always be some form of social pressure, and we will always need to free ourselves from the vanities of the modern world so as not to become the lazy, greedy, and narcissistic caricatures of modern mankind. We will always need to work toward self-mastery and social prowess so that we can authentically express who we are and joyously seek what we desire of life. Let that be our work.

A CAUSE INTERRUPTED

It is only in active self-expression and pursuit of our own aims that we can become free.

Thinking, feeling, speaking, and behaving in ways that are truly our own brings integrity and shapes the foundation for our happiness. How could we ever lose sight of this?

Seeking Personal Freedom begins when we are young and starting to form our own beliefs and directing our behaviors independent from the command of our caregivers. It is the child who takes her first steps away from her mother, who crosses the street safely by herself, who chooses with zeal what she wants to eat, wear, draw, or dress like. Hers is the story of our natural inclination to be independent, a desire to become our own persons. As we age, the impulse becomes more distinct, powerful, and intellectual—we consciously decide that we want to stand on our own, find our own way, chase our own dreams, break down our own boundaries, love without permission and contribute without restriction. We decide to go away to school, break off an affair, take a risk, start a new career, join a movement, see the world. We start asserting our ideas because we want to make our own mark. This natural impulse never goes away.

The issue is that our seeking is tragically interrupted in our lives again and again, stolen away by those around us or our own fearful thinking.

And that is the reality that we now face.

We must overcome social- and self-oppression if we are ever to join the ranks of the free souls who love their lives and lead their people.

SOCIAL OPPRESSIONS

Our most difficult task is to defeat social oppression, the caging of our spirit and the stifling of our potential by others. We mean the moments when someone exercises judgment, authority, or power against us in a burdensome, cruel, manipulative, or unjust manner. It's when a parent controls us so much that we can't be ourselves; when a lover threatens to withhold love if we don't do what they say; when a boss lies and then threatens us against telling the truth; when we want to follow our own spiritual beliefs but the culture suffocates us with its dogma. It's when any other person's petty judgments, harsh criticisms, demeaning comments, injuries, or unreasonable expectations and direct or indirect actions hold us back. When others make us feel insignificant, powerless, or unworthy, this is an effect of oppression. All the artificial barriers erected by a controlling society are part of this—the absurd informal rules or formal bureaucracies that limit people according to background, class, religion, race, ethnicity, sexual preference, age, or appearance.

Some of us can remember dramatic times when we were mocked for being different or manipulated into conformity. We can recall situations when we compromised who we were to avoid conflict. *We gave away pieces of our integrity in order to get along with others.* We started acting like "them" in school or at the office. We faked it, put on a smile, walked the path we were told to. We did all we could to avoid the silence of ostracism or the sting of their judgment. We hoped, above all, to be secure, to be accepted, to belong.

Social oppression is at work when the ways of others diminish who we are or stop us from pursuing our own goals. Often the most highly adaptive among us are the least aware of this process, and often they are socially the least successful and authentic—they have adapted into a predictable character and have lost their spontaneity and authenticity. They do not recognize themselves any longer in the mirror; they have forfeited their individuality; they are but caricatures of collective preference. No freethinking person wants such a fate, and so we must be eternally vigilant in refusing the desire to conform.

Yet the sense of security people get from conformity cannot be understated; it is one of the great enemies of Personal Freedom. The structures and rewards of society give order to an individual. But job titles, raises, "Mr." and "Mrs.," positions on advisory boards, and public acclaim rarely give us deep meaning. They can indeed make it easier to be confident in our direction. If we follow in preordained paths what others are doing, then we can get signals that we are on track and that we will likely be accepted. But what if we chase all that and believe in all that and then one day awake to find those things aren't what matter most?

To ask such a question, to rattle the cage of conformity, is to invite real risk into our lives. Once freed from the cage, an animal finds itself alone, unsure of what to do, separated from a life and things that it understands. The sudden uncertainty can be paralyzing. If we had total freedom in life, what exactly would we do, where would we go, how would we behave day-to-day, and what would give us meaning? These questions can be terrifying.

With this uncertainty there is also risk of vulnerability and loneliness. We are vulnerable because we are beyond the safe bars of the cage that, while limiting, make us feel secure. Those still trapped in the cage no longer see the freed as one of them. To refuse other's expectations may bring about our greatest fears—that we will be left isolated or abandoned, deemed inferior, thought unworthy of love.

But to stay confined by other people's rules brings about other risks. Chasing the prizes that society tells us we must want can also drive us from our true self. How many artists turned from their art because they were told they had to make money in a traditional way? How many talented people shirk their strengths to fit into a more needed but less fulfilling role? *How many have given up their dreams in order to follow a more secure and profitable and socially accepted path?* The aims of others (our parents, our teachers, our spouses, our fans) can become *our* aims if we are not vigilant. Their certitude can replace our quest for something new. Their collective meaning can subjugate our search for our individual meaning. Yes, let us be wary. We can quickly lose ourselves in others and in our culture. We become not free and genuine humans but rather slaves to opinion.

This is the ultimate misery: living a life that is not our own.

A difficult choice must therefore be made between the comforts of fitting in and pleasing others and our higher motive for Personal Freedom.

This choice is easier once we reach the levels of maturity and enlightenment that allow us to see that we can be individually free but not entirely apart from our culture and those we love, that independence does not preclude interdependence, that individual uniqueness does not mean we must be social or spiritually distant outcasts. *We learn that the more we are true to ourselves, the more we can connect with and contribute to the world.* We find that the more free and spontaneous and authentic we become, the more our motivation and aliveness returns and the more others are attracted to us and want to be around us.

SELF-OPPRESSIONS

Unfortunately, most oppression comes not from others but from a source we least suspect: ourselves.

Self-oppression is the condition of letting our own negative thoughts and actions restrict us. It is an inside job, a burdening of our spirit by incessant doubt, worry, fear, and distraction.

None of us wants to be the cause of our own failure in life—yet most often we are. It is our own inept thinking, our own bad habits that rip the vibrancy from life. We are the ultimate oppressors of our own happiness.

Self-oppression is evident whenever we limit ourselves. We stay home instead of going out because we are too anxious to explore. We procrastinate on an important assignment or exciting new venture because we cannot overcome our uncertainty. We fool ourselves into thinking that things must be perfect before we release our art into the world when the clear reality is we're just too undisciplined to get things done. We lie to ourselves, break our own resolutions, allow our dreams to slide away without grasping at them. Is it not clear to us that we can be our own worst enemy? But we can also be our own saviors. Through the active expression of our genuine nature, and the steady efforts to master our minds and move our lives forward, we can finally, after all this time, experience the freedom and joy that we deserve in life.

This is why we seek personal growth—to be *free* from the pain we cause ourselves, to make better choices, to feel better about who we are becoming, to act more confidently in social situations, and to unleash our full creativity and contributions into the world in order to make our highest difference. Gaining Personal Freedom in this sense is letting go of any self-doubt and self-loathing and allowing ourselves permission to be our unique, powerful, authentic selves.

It is in freeing ourselves to be present and genuine in life that we find trust and confidence in ourselves, that we grow and master and realize our highest selves, that we find authentic joy in our interactions and experiences in the world, that we feel motivated and liberated.

Indeed, the telltale signs that someone is free and healthy are *genuineness* and *growth*.

Aware of these things, we must have responsibility and courage to think for ourselves, to ask, "Are my ambitions, attentions, affections, and actions truly of my own choosing? Am I being my genuine self in the world and pursuing things that deeply matter to me? Am I opening myself to change and challenges so that I can stretch and grow into my full potential?"

This kind of diligence reminds us that personal power is directly tied to personal responsibility, which most people avoid. Some might hope that "freedom" means we can give up or release responsibilities from our lives, but nothing could be further from the truth. The thinking goes, "If I am free, shouldn't I be free from all responsibilities?" But Personal Freedom is not liberty to finally indulge in whatever passing moods or inclinations strike our fancy. It doesn't mean we can act on every fast need, be cruel to others around us when we feel like it, take whatever we want whenever we want it, or act as an irresponsible buffoon simply because it would be fun or pleasurable in the moment. All this would be merely slavery to unconscious impulse and compulsion.

Freedom requires responsibility to choose who we are above and beyond our immediate impulses, needs, and social pressures, so that we can genuinely express the type of person we want to be, live the life we truly want to live, leave the legacy we desire.

If we are not free to choose our character and conduct and legacy, then we are controlled by something else—thus we are lacking freedom. And if we are not responsible for our beliefs and behaviors, then someone or something else is—thus, again, we are slaves. And so the great demand is clear:

*We must be conscious and responsible
for our beliefs and behaviors
if we are ever to be free.*

Just as freedom does not mean the release of responsibility, it also does not necessarily mean the absence of struggle. To be sure, we all crave to be free from pain and limitation. But our quest for Personal Freedom is more complex. Yes, we want release from pain, but paradoxically we don't mind *adding discomfort* to our lives in order to stretch ourselves, to grow, to make a difference. We'll accept pain for gain, which is why we will push our bodies so hard to become stronger and faster, why we'll rise early despite fatigue to care for someone we love, why we'll sacrifice our time to help those in need, why we'll suffer through what is not right for a period of time to more sooner have what *is* right.

Thus Personal Freedom is more than just being free from pain—it is about being free to live, to truly enjoy and expand in life. It is not merely freedom *from* bad things that limit us, but freedom *to* experience good things that awaken us.

Long ago, the human species transcended base animal instincts; when we found reason, judgment, and intelligence, we were able to choose beyond our simple physical impulses to avoid pain or seek pleasure. We learned that meaning is more important than immediate pleasure. Indeed, what have we learned from all our mentors, heroes, teachers, survivors, leaders, saints, and legends if not that in our finest hours we are willing to forgo pleasure and endure pain in order to have freedom, meaning, love, and transcendence?

And so we want freedom from pain and yet will celebrate meaningful struggle and hardship because we know those very things will free us from one level of life and set us into another. We know that pain can be necessary and heroic, that our difficulties need not be condemned but often seen as a rite of passage that opens the doors to greatness. In this way, Personal Freedom is perhaps an enlightened and romantic ambition, heroic and poetic but real nonetheless—it is the human drive to *transcend*.

Could it be that this transcendence, this Personal Freedom, is the main motivation of mankind because it is also the ultimate demand and destination of the human experience? In our living days we strive to have more freedom of choice and prosperity so that we can genuinely express ourselves and provide more opportunities to those we love. And in our last moments, all that we have suffered for and suffered from shall be released as our souls slip into the ultimate freedom of the Divine. That is it. In life we seek Freedom; in death we are released into its vastness.

A DEDICATED PURSUIT

To achieve and sustain Personal Freedom, we must dedicate ourselves to self-mastery; we must determine and discipline our own motivations to stay true to our own sense of self, to our own path.

With this in mind, we needn't ever be confused about *why* we act the way we do. This truth is worth repeating once more, to drill it deep into our psyches so that our actions are no longer accidental or such a frustrating mystery: Every decision and action of humankind stems from a hope to attain Personal Freedom. We seek to be free from hardship, pain, fear, anxiety, and want; free from oppression; free to be ourselves; free in the moment to sense surprise, spontaneity, and our own spirit; free to choose our life's course; free to pursue our dreams; free to love openly without judgment or condition or regret; free to give our time and energy and resources to causes we believe in; free to experience and enjoy future peace, passions, and prosperity. It is the primary motive for all our striving: *to be free.*

If we can remember that it is Personal Freedom we seek, then we can organize, aim, and realize ourselves. And so let us now be fully conscious of Personal Freedom as our driving force and let us remember to honor that drive in our daily ambitions and actions. Let freedom ring in our ears once more, this time more loudly, more closely, more personally. Let us be bold in our self-expression and dedicated in building our ideal lives.

There is no veil of ease about the extraordinary effort required to be free. Breaking from conformity and pursuing our own dreams will bring some discord upon us. There will be personal struggle and sacrifice, fear and misfortune, as we try to exert ourselves in the world once more. A vital dedication to our genuine nature and our dreams will annoy people or raise their ire; it will injure egos, step on toes, split relationships, and force interventions with those who try to limit us or stop our march. We might have to confront the bullies, break up with the jerks, leave the poisonous work environment, and challenge others to higher standards.

Yes, this work will be hard. So let us take stock of what lies ahead. This work will require that we finally declare who we are and what we want. It will require new levels of presence and power and ownership in the important roles we play in our lives. It will require us to upend our very days and, finally, reestablish personal control of our agenda. It will require the courage to defeat the internal demons that defy our greatness. It will require the will-

ingness to advance with abandon beyond our own comfort zones. It will require new practices of joy and a greater
sense of gratitude. It will require that we refuse to break
our integrity when faced with hardship. It will require that
we unleash love so that our soul can soar. It will require a
rise to greatness so that we may serve and lead and leave
our mark. And it will require that we sense time differently
so that we might experience each moment's vastness and
freedom. For each of these efforts we must set bold new
declarations in our lives.

To spend the full force of our energies advancing toward
a Personal Freedom—the genuine life full of vibrancy and
meaning—*this* shall be our aim. Let us marshal our motivations to align with such a high and worthy cause. Let
us set new declarations and discipline in our life. Let the
value of freedom ring through every crevice of our minds,
through every thought and action we choose, through
every relationship we influence, through the long days and
long marches that lead to our highest selves and highest
contributions, through all the hopeful dreams born from a
liberated soul.

2

ON FEAR

———

He who is brave is free.

SENECA

FEAR RIPS US FROM FREEDOM. IT IS THE DESTROYER OF greatness. We know this, and we know we should tame our mind in order to defeat fear. Yet look at all the adults who act like powerless children and avoid the life they want because of fear. The socially oppressed say, "Well, you don't understand. People are always holding me back, and I am afraid to chase my dreams because others will judge and reject me." And the self-oppressed say, "You don't understand. I can't chase my dreams because I might fail—I might not be good enough." These are the debilitating thoughts of the fearful. Should we wish to live a vibrant life, we must transcend such childishness and look fear in the eye, recognizing it as a mental construct that we alone fuel with small thoughts that betray our magnitude.

It is the first realization of the mindful human: Unless we are being chased by a deadly animal or deranged human, or face imminent physical harm like falling to our death, fear is just bad management of our mind.

Today we are faced with a multitude of placaters and licensed professionals, many of whom have never actually transformed lives, who try to fool us into believing fear is a positive emotion in life. They say, "Fear is natural," or "A little fear will motivate you to try harder," or "Fear builds character." But in most cases, this is wrong. Fear is the thief of humanity's light. It may be a necessary instinct that causes us to make smart choices to flee from pain, danger, or struggle, but we must be wary of it. More people find harm in life because of fear than benefit by it. Those who seek to make fear a positive thing are justifiers, not sages. They aren't champions of consciousness. Attempting to conceal fear as a friend is like forcing a wolf to be a pet. Soon the pet will eat us alive.

Declaring that we will master our fears is the first great leap toward freedom. Our vitality, growth, and destiny all demand that we can topple fear. As so much hangs in the balance, let us better understand what fear really is.

Fear is the human motive of *aversion*. Fear doesn't help us commit to higher aims. It doesn't help us imagine greatness. Its sole aim is immediate release from threat, strain, or pain. It often becomes a by-all-means-necessary approach to controlling any given situation so that the body—but most often the ego—can feel safe and unchallenged.

Fear was given to us as a motive to avoid physical harm and death. That is it. *We are the ones who have perverted it into a tool for the ego's protection.* Almost all the fear we experience today has *nothing* to do with physical threat. We have taken this impulse for safety and bastardized it into ego-driven desires to feel more emotionally comfortable. We've hacked its short-term nature into a long-term tool to avoid difficult circumstances in order to satiate our base desires for approval. Fear has become a crutch for emotional weakness. And as with all crutches, we shall fall slave to its use unless we once more condition our strength.

Most people do not like to discuss fear because it inevitably exposes the ugly truth that we are more often fleeing from ourselves than from actual danger. The modern worries that we succumb to are simply by-products of our own misuse of this primitive motive. Almost all fear we experience today, and its resultant cowardly thinking and behavior, is just imagined *social drama* created by *unchecked* mental impulses and conditionings. We are afraid of being rejected, isolated, or abandoned—not of being eaten alive. And those kinds of social fears can be overcome by willful practice.

When someone says, "I am fearful of public speaking," they do not mean that they are worried someone in the audience is going to attack them physically. Rather, they mean they are afraid of failure. Their issue is a challenge not of real safety but of *emotional comfort*. If they were speaking more accurately, they would say, "I am afraid of how I will feel emotionally, and whether I will live up to my expectations of myself and the expectations of those who put me on stage. I am afraid of how I will look. I am afraid that I may not do well. I am afraid I will lose my place or draw a blank; I am afraid I will not be respected." Notice the order of these comments. It is not "Fear is running me"; it is "*I* am afraid." The "I" is leading the way—the ego is in charge.

Naturally, we all struggle with free self-expression, and we all want to do our best. We would love the power to be ourselves on the world's stage at all times. Our great challenge is that in an unconditioned mind, fear is louder and more intense and immediate than our desire for self-mastery or for contribution to others. Fear steals thunder from the more noble drive to ascend to our highest selves and make our greatest difference. We are more alert to the sound of dogs barking than angels singing. What can be done?

THE COST OF FEAR

To tame fear we must first recognize its horrid effects on our lives. What comes of us when we are motivated by fear? We lose our emotional center and mental character. Our thoughts become frazzled and riddled with anxiety. All conscious thinking, intelligence, and behavior narrow to self-protection, limiting our capabilities to be open and strong. Our natural tendencies for genuine self-expression are paused, and our ability to act to fulfill our dreams is paralyzed. When we *allow* fear as a constant in our lives, our ambitions and behaviors become small and constrained. We become timid and stressed. We withdraw. We become cowards. Life's energy entropies—all things trapped in the cage of fear smother and die quickly.

This is not a philosophical discussion. Real, tangible harm comes from allowing fear to overrule our drive to Personal Freedom. Some people become such slaves to fear that they constantly feel powerless, inferior, ready to give up.

They allow others to hurt them because they do not speak up for themselves. They quietly play it safe, never showing themselves to the world. These are the meek who stood to inherit the earth but never rose to claim it; the sullen who watched atrocities wear on without a word of defiance. Good people stand at the sidelines of history and never make their mark. People lose their businesses because fear stops them from changing and innovating. Marriages end in divorce because one or both spouses are too afraid to open up, to communicate, to be vulnerable or sexy or honest.

On a societal level, all the worst atrocities of mankind stem from fear. Those compelled by fear become terrified, distrustful, and often hateful of other people. Their fear gives rise to an overweening self-protection to such a degree that they want power over others. Their ego is so fiercely challenged by the rise of people unlike themselves that they become the bigots and tyrants and sometimes grand-scale murderers whose unchecked fear burns into a perilous soup of unspeakable actions against humanity. These are the Caligulas, Mussolinis, and Bin Ladens of the world, who hate others because they fear those who stand in their way to power. They are the Robespierres, Eichmanns, Sungs, and Khomenis; the Hitlers, Stalins, and Amins. It's the same story over and over again: those with power who are so plagued by insecurity that, rather than directing their strengths to lift everyone up, take comfort and pleasure in pushing down those who are unlike themselves, those they do not understand or value.

There can be no doubt that whether in daily life or on the world's stage, fear is the great usurper of progress and Personal Freedom. It is a sad but real fact that history is littered with good men and women who simply *let* the motive of fear drive their lives. Nothing ever cued them to right their mind, or they never chose to work hard to condition their thoughts to tame fear, to choose consciousness over the ease of running away from life.

AVERSION VS. ASCENSION

Fear rules us only if we let it. In almost all cases, it is something that we can choose to activate or not activate. We can choose to run or not, even if our impulse is blaring at its highest decibel to run. How else does the firefighter enter the inferno to save people? How does the captain of a ship give the lifeboats to the others? How do the anxious still share their voice with the world? Perhaps we don't *feel* like we can make this choice to be more brave than fearful, but eventually we can all become masters of our impulses.

> *A great maturity opens in the human psyche*
> *when we accept that we can control*
> *our impulses by conditioning our thoughts,*
> *and that we alone are responsible*
> *for our emotions and reactions in life.*

It is difficult to accept but no less true: If fear is winning in our lives, it is because we simply keep choosing it over our other impulses to be strong or bold or great. This is the story of the stay-at-home mom who wants to go back to work but didn't apply because she is letting her fear of her own worth hold her back. It's the employee who wants to ask for a deserved raise but feels afraid she might be denied. It's the young man who feels inspired to try out for a musical but worries what his friends will think. It's the obese person too embarrassed to enter the gym even though he knows his health and very existence is on the line.

Most adults understand that they are making a choice to let fear win in any given situation. Ask an honest person, "Did you know you were acting from fear the last time you stopped behaving as yourself or working toward something you wanted, and did you know *you had another choice* at the time?" The honest person will say, "Yes. I knew I had a chance to speak up for myself or to be more courageous. But I was scared. I didn't want to be judged or hurt, so I chose the easy route."

Let us be clear once more that if we are not free, if we are not genuinely expressing our full personality and pursuing our true desires, it is because we are choosing to act from aversion rather than ascension. Thus our grand battles in life are between our desire for freedom and the fearful impulses that destroy desire. The juxtaposition could be no less stark—*at any moment, we are acting from a state of mind driven by fear or freedom.* And the stakes are high: all advancement in our maturity and growth as individuals and societies hinges on our motives. Either fear will win or freedom will win. Let that phrase ring true in our minds as we carry out our ideal lives:

Fear wins or Freedom wins.

And so let us ask ourselves, *"Will my life be about aversion or ascension?"* The former is a life motivated by fear, a small life that turns from hardship toward short-term safety,

self-protection, and egotistic ease. The other is a life motivated by freedom, a reason to act from our true humanity
toward long-term growth, authentic self-expression, and
enlightened effort. One is the conditioning of weak and
constrained and conforming and suffering beings; the other
the conditioning of strong, spontaneous, independent,
and fulfilled beings. One reaches us as a lowly and often
pathetic impulse; the other requires our full consciousness
and mental devotion to courage and self-mastery.

THE SOCIAL CONDITIONING OF FEAR

Why are some people more driven by fear than freedom?

It can only be because in the past they were conditioned
to be fearful, either by those around them or by their poor
application of mental faculties. There is no genetic curse or
personality trait that permanently condemns one person to
fear more than another—even a genetic predisposition for
anxiety can ultimately be flipped on or off by mental conditioning. *We are not slave to our history; we can be freed by our
conscious thoughts and disciplined habits.*

Let us begin with understanding how fear is socially conditioned. Fearful people tend to be shaped by past interactions.
They were pushed and molded into being timid, weak, and
afraid by the critical parents, bullying peers, or small-minded
teachers and bosses. The people around them were always cau-
tioning or harming them, and so they became habituated to
the impulse of fear—it came up so often they got used to it.
From a fearful past they have generated a fear-driven present.

This is not to blame our past or excuse our fears. When people choose fear as an adult, they are choosing not to manage or overcome it. This is difficult work for many because fear has become their default impulse. The thoughts ruling their minds and their self-talk replay the cutting barbs of the critics and misguided caretakers who once demeaned them. The good news is we can change this conditioning. When we awaken to responsibility, we realize that nothing can be done about our past but to see it from a new perspective. We can release ourselves from its grip. We cannot control how others treated us yesterday, so let us work instead on understanding how we are currently dealing with those who stoke our fear today. The great efforts to move our lives forward always come down to a new moment when we interrupt our fear and activate our freedom by choosing how to feel, interpret, and direct our lives.

Part of the mastery of life comes from anticipating that the same kinds of characters that sought to instill fear yesterday shall be met again today or tomorrow. Knowing this, we become wary of people who chip away at our freedom. These are the worriers, weaklings, and, in rare cases, the wicked.

The Worriers

The *worriers* around us today are often the biggest threat to enflaming our fear. They are the most likely to steal our motivation and destiny because they often seem to be our friends. We are so close to them that their anxiety can bleed onto us. We must learn to control our reactions around them.

Most worriers are not unkind people. They have no clue of the fear they impose on our lives, or the way their incessant voices of doubt oppress our potential. They don't see that they cause treachery by arguing for us to play it safe. It's the loving mother who says, "Careful, honey," at every turn as her child goes about the normal activities of childhood; the coworker who gives ten reasons why we might get in trouble and not a single word about how we might change the world; the lover who incessantly fears we as a couple are going to fail and keeps imploring us to back down from a fight or from the edge of any risk.

These people believe they are thoughtful, loving, and protective. Their cautious words are most often delivered from a loving place. They want good for us. They feel a duty to protect us from hurt, and so they try to direct us toward the well-worn paths that they understand. These are our parents, friends, peers, lovers, neighbors, and leaders.

It's an awkward social reality: *We must protect ourselves from being limited by those who care for us as much as by those who blatantly oppose us.*

What can be done? We must learn to hear doubt, worry, and anxiety with great acuity, and we must not integrate other people's fears into our own decision making. Developing this kind of acuity is easy for the conscious person, since almost all worriers use the same language and arguments—they favor *cautioned reason* as their shield of choice in "protecting" us. Their matter-of-fact tones and phrases all sound the same:

"Be careful; you might get hurt."

"Be careful; you don't know what could happen."

"Be careful; they might fire you, forget you, reject you, hate you, spurn you, despise you, pick on you."

"Are you sure you want to do that?"

"You wouldn't like that."

"That's not who you are."

"You can't do this."

"That's not really your thing."

Have we not heard all this before? Surely we all know someone adept at crafting eloquent arguments for why we mustn't be too loud, too crazy, too intent on pursuing our passion or taking too many leaps into the unknown. These are the calm and convincing ones in our lives—those who present clear-eyed explanations about how we could be hurt, embarrassed, or exhausted if we take risks or try to be different, creative, alive, bold.

These people are clearly not callous. They believe they are doing their duty. They seem motherly and judicious, working with great care to protect us. But let us beware the saboteur of dreams cloaked in the goodwilled friend. How many souls have failed to soar because they were suffocated in a loved one's worry?

If we are not vigilant, being around constant worry can quickly limit who we are and what we might be capable of. What can we do, then, with our caring families and friends who unintentionally limit our vision or striving?

We should be generous in our interpretations of their concern, as they are likely unaware of their insidious effect, which is to teach us to at first consider risk or harm before all else. We must harbor no ill feelings toward these worriers; they deserve patience and understanding because they may be trapped in a mindset that favors aversion over ascension. Let them be governed by fear if they must, but do not join them.

All we can do is listen intently to those we *trust*, and be sober in our estimates of any real danger. But to those who we do not know, and who do not know *us*, to those who want us to stay put in their bubble of belief about who we are and how far we can go in life, we must close our minds. We must forgive their small thinking and we must look beyond it to see a vaster horizon for ourselves. *We must not worry what could go wrong but rather wonder what magnificence could enter our lives when we are consistently expressing our genuine selves and pursuing our true passions.*

Let us obsess about freedom, not fear.

And so a deep line must be cut into the sand: *There can be no tolerance for worriers in life.* All great men and women come to this same determined conclusion. No matter how kindhearted the deliverer, we cannot give prolonged consideration to those who repeatedly instill fear in us. It demotivates and demoralizes.

When our dreams become vivid and enliven us, we must venture forth, with or without worried family and friends, even if it brings some sorrow and sacrifice. To allow other people's anxieties to defeat our drive is to succumb to oppression.

The Weaklings

The next category of people we must anticipate are the weak and slothful, those who speak out against the efforts and hardships required to be remarkable.

It would be too simple to say, "Do not give your ear to a lazy person, as he will surely pour fear and apathy into your soul." But it is nonetheless a powerful mantra. Choosing *not* to listen to weaklings demands true personal power, especially for those of us who are good listeners and empathetic friends, as we want to respect their opinions and circumstances. We must be discerning with those we know well and allow close; it is possible to listen lovingly while being careful about what energy we absorb.

With strangers, it makes sense to be guarded: it is easy to be seduced by bon vivants and those who promise lazy afternoons of eating, drinking, gossiping, or watching tasteless reality. We can be fooled by their leisurely pace, mistaking their lack of ambition for serenity. But these kinds of people can be more apathetic than relaxed. We must beware them, for they can make us fear the thing that advances our lives: *effort*.

"*Take it easy*," they say. "Why work so hard? Nothing you do is going to last or mean anything or make a difference anyway."

It's as though on our ambitious journey, these people wave toward us on the sidelines with a smile, yet they whisper to others that our toils are a waste of time. They make like watchmen, warning us with great glee against oncoming struggles.

But the closer to these idlers that we pass, the more we hear them silently joking at our expense, demeaning our efforts, criticizing our comrades in struggle. Beware the raucous village idiot who takes pleasure in making faraway jabs, taunting the strivers passing by, hoping to instill the fear of unworthiness.

Who are these idlers? They are worshippers of ease who rarely feel the satisfaction of a hard day's work. They are the aimless souls who pursue no real path, no purpose, no higher desire that would demand the best of them. They may never have found the courage to abandon complacency. They are glib cynics who have added little real value to the world. They are the escapists, those who bolt away at the first inkling of a challenge. They scorn the presence of those bolder than they. They are fatalists who believe that mankind's star is not rising but sinking. They are the resigned, the miserable few who long ago gave up their power so that they might be absolved of the responsibility of living a remarkable life.

We mustn't take these loiterers on the sidelines for friends. These people will inspire nothing but weakness, and their invitations to a life of ease are lures to a life of indolence. Their ease is not what we are after. For what good is a life without struggle? What can be learned? How else do we grow? What mastery can there be without real effort, real sweat, real toil, real thunder?

Yes, we should meet with caution the apathetic and unambitious, those too weak to fight or try or endure. They have forfeited their freedom. They don't have the resolve to pursue their highest selves or any meaningful purpose. And so they are not examples for us.

What a great irony that humans often follow the weakest among us—the cynics and the trolls. But we mustn't give these weak fools our time either. We must understand that the lowest rung of humanity is populated by the couch critics, the apathetic advisors who, from a detached perch of safety, believe that every whim that breezes over their small minds, and every one of their witless arguments, ought to carry the same weight as the hard-won wisdom of those who are actually in the fight, whose minds have been sharpened with real-world experience, whose legends are being forged by action. We must remember that most cynics and judgmental tyrants who seek to oppress us are small, frustrated people who take the heat off their own apathy and failure by labeling us as narcissistic strivers or undeserving fakes. They try to belittle us to stop feeling so little themselves. These are those who hide behind a computer or powerful position and exert their uninformed opinion on us so that they feel better about themselves. Should they be asked about their own contributions, they generally fall silent or lash out in incoherent and meaningless diatribes. Theirs is a sad fate, where their only sense of success is to point out our failures; to elevate themselves they must demean us. Their jabs are sad demonstrations that nothing is easier for small minds than to discount great ones. For those who dwell in Ignorance, everyone from out of town is suspect.

Beware those too apathetic to strive for important things as they ultimately instill indifference, swaying so many independent people from their path of greatness. And so let us stay on our path. Let us choose the strenuous life, taking pride and finding honor in our struggles and our contributions. We will not fear the exhaustion and anxieties that magnificent dreams and unceasing hard work can bring. We will keep a joyous heart even as we toil, for our toils bring us toward that which we find meaningful. Let us humbly pass by the watchers and the aimless, the bored and the bellyaching. They have nothing to offer but distraction and useless comment.

Let us make ours a higher cause than comfort, a greater calling than mediocrity. We have duties to complete, initiatives to begin, battles to fight, real victories to celebrate. And so forward we go with strength and fire.

The Wicked

As we anticipate the weak-willed, let us also anticipate that woven in the tapestry of human goodness are also threads of mean, power-hungry, deceptive individuals. We cannot avoid the cruel people we will encounter in life—the more of them coming at us, the more we put ourselves out there, the more we seek to lead, the more we express ourselves and our full potential, the more we are motivated to change the world. The more we rise, the more they turn up.

This is not some kind of paranoia. The fact that there are mean people in the world is not something to fear; it is simply something to acknowledge and prepare for. Businesspeople should not be shocked that the competition will seek to destroy them. No surprise should flash across the face of a new executive when she is met with resistance during her first meeting simply because she is a woman. When a stranger lies to hurt our reputation, we should know that it is a common thing, and that it is happening to us only because we are trying to do important things in the world. If we are conscious to the existence of rude, ignorant, cruel people, then we can control our reaction when they emerge from the darkness and attempt to steal our light.

A society so afflicted by *ease* and *conformity* always flinches at the arrival of those boldly seeking Personal Freedom. As we express our true selves and advance toward our dreams, we will meet unfathomable, unending resistance. Those who play a zero-sum game of life—who believe they cannot succeed if we do—may launch slings and arrows of envy. Or they might seek, with soft and duplicitous words, to lull us back into the fold. Those at our sides may stab us with doubts about our readiness or warn that the world is too hostile a place. And those in front of us, fearful of losing their place, may hurl wicked accusations and build walls to keep us back. We must ready ourselves and be wary of the effect such tyrants can have in making us feel fearful in life.

We must be especially vigilant in our reactions to contemptuous, small-minded people who fight for overt and oppressive power over others: the brute who towers over others, using his physical presence to intimidate, the greedy liar at work who seeks to wreck us, the abusive lover, the vicious neighborhood gossip, the condescending bullies and the sweet-talking con artists. While we mustn't let these few tar the goodwill of the majority, we are wise not to deny their existence.

This sort of extreme tyrant has a vast terrain of ego to defend. They can be narcissistic, paranoid, angry people. Their commonality is that they are on constant search for those seeking their level of success. They want to wreck them. Their goal is to oppress our will and energy so that they can feel better about themselves. Consciously or unconsciously, they see our advance as a threat to their power or a sign of their weakness. And so if they can minimize us, they can minimize their loss of stature.

We see this sort of tyrant often at the helm of struggling countries, protecting interests with a fearful hand, enslaving people and ostracizing dissidents. We see them in the corridors of commercial success, lording over their underlings, wielding harsh criticism or rumor, denying the advancement of the deserving. They are often family members, battering the very ones who depend on them. All their taunts and threats and terrors function to make us fear for our safety, security, or prosperity so that we might fall in line with their demands.

Of all their ways to hurt us, belittling our worth is the tyrant's most vicious weapon. "You are unworthy, stupid, inadequate, unskilled," they tell us. Their harsh words and actions seek to box us into their concept of who we are and where we belong. The effect? We start to fear that we are not good enough or cannot win, and tragically this can quickly become a self-fulfilling prophesy. We can come to believe we are as small as they tell us we are, and we can choose to stay in their pathetic boundaries of belief rather than roam freely into our own freedom.

We should not be surprised when others demean or resist our initiatives. Nor should we suppress our will and let them win. We mustn't let the wicked stoke our doubts into the mighty flames of fear that consume our dreams.

To these tyrants, we owe nothing.

A truly oppressive person cannot see beyond his or her own self-interest and so no relationship with them will ever be joyful or reciprocal. They are blinded by their ego and live in a world by themselves and for themselves. Do not grovel to these people. Do not try to placate them. Do not hope they will change. Do not engage with them or hang about with them. Do not let them provoke anger. *Never sink to their level.* We must never tolerate a tyrant's efforts to hold us back. We mustn't let them govern our potential. Every display of submission, deference, meekness, and compromise they see from the desperate or feeble among us gives them a perverse joy, and their power grows. And every time we back down from them or minimize ourselves, we become more fearful and weak.

So let us be diligent in avoiding these people, without ever deviating from our own path. We mustn't wish them ill; it's not worth the energy, and wicked people will get what they deserve as they destroy themselves. Our success lies not in their destruction but in our own advancement, not in the astonishment on their faces as we surge past them but in the joy in our hearts at having prevailed despite them.

THE MENTAL PROJECTION OF FEAR

While many people in our lives might seek to stoke our doubts and fears, the vast majority will seek to support us. More will seek to pull us up than push us down. People know that in allowing us to chase our dreams unencumbered, they are silently giving themselves permission to pursue their own. No matter how many bores and bastards we meet in life, we must remember that we have friends all around, and we mustn't hesitate to ask for their help, inspiration, and wisdom.

The hard truth of life is that though our fear is often socially cued and conditioned, it is more often a result of dereliction of our own minds. We *misuse* our mental faculties by barely *using* them at all. We have the means to extinguish our fears, but we lack discipline in using it, like having the extinguisher in our hands as our home burns but choosing not to use it because we'd have to aim. How often do we sense worry but, rather than combatting it with conscious thought, let it burn? How often do we so obsess on negative things that they grow into a great scorching fire of anxiety? For many people, this has happened unchecked so often and for so long that they are no longer aware of the fact that *predictable thought patterns*—all of which they can anticipate and control and transform—are causing them to be fearful. They just feel afraid all the time and think there is nothing they can do about it, like a sad child holding a burst balloon she herself popped.

Let us learn now, once and for all, to anticipate how our minds cultivate fear. Just as we can expect the worriers, weaklings, and wicked to derail us if we are not cautious, we can prepare for how our minds will tear us from happiness and progress.

Most of the fear we feel in life is simply anxiety arising from our anticipation of two kinds of pain that change might bring: the pain associated with *loss* or *hardship*.

The first type, loss pain, is a thought pattern in which we worry that we will lose something we cherish if we take any given action. If we fear changing jobs, it is because we don't want to lose our compensation, our friendships with certain coworkers, our corner office. This thought pattern plays out in millions of subtle decisions throughout people's lives. We think, "If I go on a new diet, I'm afraid I'll lose the joy I feel in eating my favorite foods." "If I quit smoking, I'll lose that 20 minutes of peace I get by going outside and taking long drags, so I'm afraid to quit." "If I leave the jerk, I'm afraid I'll lose love in my life and never find anyone else to be with."

The only way to combat this thought pattern is to analyze it closely, then *reverse* it. Once we sense that we are anticipating loss, we must question whether or not it is true.

The more we look for evidence of our fears, the more we realize they are often faulty, quick assumptions of a tired or undirected mind.

The small, poorly conditioned person may guess that things will be bad whereas an intelligent, self-aware person may come to a logical conclusion based on real-world evidence or thoughtful principle. The person who examines their fear of dieting, quitting a bad habit, or leaving a bad relationship comes to realize there is always less to lose than to gain in making healthy decisions for themselves.

This reframing requires intelligence—and optimism. Once we question the assumptions causing us anxiety, we should explore the opposite of our worries, focusing as obsessively as possible on what might be *gained* if we changed. What if we begin the new diet and find new foods and recipes we love? What if we quit smoking and learn new practices that give us even more relaxation? What if, in a new romantic relationship, we finally find joy? We should certainly visualize these outcomes as much as we visualize dark scenes of loss. Dream up and focus on the positive, for it is much more useful than the long nightmares of negativity.

The second thought pattern that causes us to fear change is related to the anticipation of hardship. We're scared to do something because we think it will be too hard on us. We worry we're not capable, worthy, or ready, and we allow that worry to stop us. But isn't this a pathetic use of mental powers? *Isn't it true that with enough time, effort, and dedication we can learn most of what we need to succeed?* Isn't it true that most great accomplishments were achieved by people who at first had *no idea what they were doing,* who had to first endure years of struggle to bring their dream to fruition? Let's not forget that we didn't always know how to ride a bike or use a computer or make love, but we figured it out. Humans did not know how to land on the moon, but we decided it was a worthwhile endeavor, and so we struggled for a decade to puzzle it out. We became capable of the impossible. Thus is the story of the individual and the entire species.

And yet look how small we let our minds be in so many cases. We think, "I'm scared to go on a diet because I don't know if I can handle learning all these new recipes fast enough or endure a 30-minute workout." "I'm afraid of quitting smoking because it will be hard to know what to do with my hands without a cigarette in them." "I'm too freaked out to leave my bad relationship because going online to find someone new sounds like a hassle." We are more than these small thoughts. At some point, maturity will pounce on us and ask, *"Are you not more than your tiny worries about inconvenience? Isn't a better life worth some struggle?"*

The only way to break these thought patterns is to question and reverse them. If we simply take a moment to contemplate, we can realize we have learned and endured more difficult things in the past, and we can learn and endure what is needed now. *The tools to manage the difficulties of life are within.* Perhaps we can imagine ourselves actually enjoying the struggle versus fearing it. We can think, "I'm looking forward to learning to cook new foods. I'm looking forward to working out with my friends." "I'm excited to quit smoking because I can see myself getting up the stairs without being winded, and having a long life free of addiction." "I'm thrilled to look for someone who is more right for me than my last relationship, to find real love, to enjoy life with my soul mate." Let us fire our enthusiasm knowing that the learning journey toward freedom can be exciting. We must trust this: *We can learn and we can grow and we must begin now for destiny favors the bold.*

To some, this sounds like mere positive thinking. And what of it? Shall we continue thinking negatively? What good will come from focusing on all the loss and hardship we might experience in life? There is no self-awareness in letting fear reign because of our own mental sloth. We have the personal power to wield our thoughts more forcefully in the daily fight against our fears. Our thoughts will free us or destroy us. Maturity comes in understanding that it is our choice alone to move toward freedom.

DEALING WITH PHYSICAL FEAR

It seems impossible that all our fears can be conquered by mindset alone. But they can be. Some ask, "What about those real physical impulses that seem so uncontrollable? Can we also master them?"

How does the lion tamer walk into the pride's den unafraid? How does the public speaker stand in front of thousands without becoming ill with self-doubt? How does the executive make the decision her whole team is too afraid to make?

Practice. The lion tamer was once afraid. But he entered the den, and over time he became unafraid. The public speaker took the stage, and with time became comfortable. The executive made decision after decision until even the big calls became easier. We can learn from these examples and choose to face what we fear. *We can choose the courage to put ourselves in the vicinity of the things we fear over and over again until we grow more comfortable and then confident.*

Let us reawaken to a life unbounded, finding inspiration in the fact that humans throughout the millennia have learned to overcome their fears. They changed how they reacted to fearful impulses. They took a deep breath, contemplated whether or not their fears were rational, and visualized the growth they would experience by moving forward. They took those steps forward again and again until they found that their fear was no longer so powerful or even present. This is called self-mastery. Let us learn from them and put these practices into our own lives. Let us choose to master our minds and demonstrate more power over our fears.

As mature and bold adults, we can refuse to shrink from those things that might cause us anxiety or hardship. We can reach toward what is always pulsing in the background, that equally powerful impulse, that sure and solid will toward Personal Freedom. We repeat over and over: "I won't let others stoke fear in my heart. I choose to remain true to who I am and where my dreams direct me no matter the hardship I might incur. I remember it always: Fear wins or Freedom wins, and I choose Freedom."

3

ON MOTIVATION

If you want to build a ship,
don't drum up people together to collect wood and don't
assign them tasks and work, but rather teach them
to long for the endless immensity of the sea.

ANTOINE DE SAINT-EXUPÉRY

THE DOMINANT MOTIVES OF HUMANKIND INVOLVE either freedom or fear; there are no other pathways in our psychology. One demands engagement with our true self and ambitions, and inevitably leads to independence, growth, happiness, and transcendence. The other causes us to skirt around challenges, avoiding struggle as much as possible—despite struggle often being the very thing required for growth. This path leads to weakness, conformity, and, frequently, regret. Through the pursuit of Personal Freedom, we discover our destiny; through fear, we look at our demise.

Our reasons for tapping into these motives are often called our *motivation*. We can feel motivated to move forward or to halt, to grow or to shrink, to settle or to chase greatness. The actions we take in life are often based on whether our internal logic and impulses lean toward fear or freedom. If we lack compelling reasons to take action, or if our impulses are fearful or protective, then we tend to stay put. But if we have a strong list of reasons to move forward and we've conditioned our impulses to support freedom, we are more likely to consistently advance our lives.

With freedom on the line, we would expect that most of us would understand how motivation works in our lives. But many remain clueless, reacting to each day of life without reason or power. Thus they are not free—they are slaves to impulse. And that is why we have so many people trapped in aimlessness, apathy, and fear. Motivation remains a mystery to the masses.

Yet the first virtue of the great among us is a remarkable level of *sustained motivation.* Success and fulfillment in life rests on the unflagging ability to get up, to be ourselves, to chase our dreams with fire each day, to keep willing ourselves to the next level of presence and performance and potential. More broadly, our entire human value system rests on motivation. *None* of the great human values that keep us and society in check—kindness, love, honesty, fairness, unity, tolerance, respect, responsibility—would flourish if we were not *motivated* to bring them to life. And so if we fail to master our motivation at an individual level, we cannot be happy; if we fail to maintain our motives for goodness at a societal level, all would be lost.

What great heights could we reach if we truly activated our human motivation? Imagine how the world would change, almost immediately, if its citizens could turn on their motivation whenever desired, for as long as desired. Would more people become free and happy? Would we have the stamina to end poverty? Would we build more schools? Might we end famine, eliminate dis-ease, free those wrongly imprisoned, stop global warming, and achieve remarkable progress in every corner of the globe? Would billions more see their dreams come true?

How different our society could be if true motivation ran deep, if all that apathy and aimlessness drifted away and our people were fired by a conscious mind and a consistently committed heart? Imagine how the world would prosper. Imagine the freedom.

This is a reachable possibility because motivation is stunningly simple to figure out and act upon. And so let us begin that path by demystifying *why* we do what we do.

THE MOTHER OF MOTIVATION

Our first step is to understand motivation's root, *motive*, which means *a reason for action*. It's the "why" we do something. To develop a motive for action, our mind, with or without conscious guidance, filters through various thoughts, feelings, and experiences, and *chooses* from them a set of reasons to do or not do something. Our mind's clarity on and commitment to that choice dictates our level of motivation. If we are clear and committed, we will feel high levels of motivation. If we are unclear or uncommitted, motivation will be low. From this process comes a simple axiom:

The mother of motivation is choice.

Our mind *chose* a reason for action, and it either committed to that choice or it did not, and thus we experience a high level of motivation or a low one. In this truth we find our greatest personal power: the ability to take over our impulses and direct our minds to choices and commitments that will serve us.

Simply, we can choose our aim, and our reasons for that aim, and a continued focus on the aim will arouse a desire for action, which we sense as energy—a motivating power within.

A hallmark of those who achieve greatness
is the discovery that they can control
the level of motivation they feel
by better directing their own minds.

This is true for other emotional breakthroughs as well. Enlightenment comes when we realize happiness is a choice, sadness is a choice, anger is a choice, love is a choice. Every state, emotion, and mood available to Man can be generated at will in our mind. This realization is one of the most obvious guideposts on the path from adolescence to adulthood, from immaturity to maturity, from terror in life to transcendence.

This is not to say that *all* people can or will choose their thoughts or emotions. A small percentage of the public does not have the faculties of a healthy mind; clinical mood and mental disorders can prevent people from consciously directing their own thoughts and feelings on a consistent basis. Therapy and medication can help in such cases, and should be sought. We must not discount the challenges faced by those with real disorders and biological issues that prevent their progress in life.

Though the vast swath of the population does *not* suffer from such clinical disorders, they may show a lack of self-awareness as well as poor mental habits. *Most people have simply not yet chosen to prize self-mastery or to work toward it.* They do not need drugs; they need desire and discipline. They do not need a prescription; they need a new life philosophy. Even in those cases where a person needs medication and therapy over the long term, their treatment will also almost always include efforts to help them choose thoughts and behaviors that better support their well-being. Even in mental illness or traumatic brain injury, all roads of recovery lead to better understanding and directing our own minds. If we become cynics and decide it is too difficult for us or anyone to control our mind, then we are destined to forever drift in a sea of impulses and social cues, a life of reaction and distraction rather than one of conscious design.

The long evolutions of philosophy, psychology, and neuroscience share a common theme of unlocking human potential by leveraging *reason* and the full power of the mind. Reason is the secret to developing a motivated and independent identity. *I* think *therefore I am and I do.* Motivated people seize this truth. The great artists, leaders, and innovators use the entire force of their reasoning faculties to become their highest selves and do their highest good. They express who they truly are and pursue goals they find meaningful. They strategically contemplate their direction and values; they weigh what will give them the greatest sense of vibrancy and fulfillment in every major decision. They select from life's abundant array only the courses that suit their nature and their intention to be free and to serve. They are resolute in calling forth their greatest character traits and wrestling their lowest impulses into submission. They appear, in the eyes of the mindless masses, to be the lucky ones, the chosen. In fact, they decided to *choose*.

People who are motivated are not lucky. They are *conscientious*. They choose to use their minds in a more purposeful way in order to energize and lift their lives. And for that they tend to achieve more and gain more respect. The thoughtful woman, who is in charge of her own mind and emotions, has extraordinary power and earns high regard. But the man not in charge of his own mind is lost in a swirl of unpredictable and often unwanted thoughts and impulses. He is seen as immature or unreliable, and as the vacuum of his unconscious fills with fear, he inevitably drowns in self-doubt or suffers social despair.

When we understand that thoughts and emotions can be chosen, then we finally realize that we err in saying, *"I don't feel happy"* or *"I feel sad and there is nothing I can do about it."* Since we have some choice in how we feel at any given moment, the more accurate statements would be *"I am not using my mind right now to generate a feeling of happiness"* or *"I have been choosing to focus on sad things for a while and that has created this feeling of sadness"* or *"I am allowing my unconscious impulses to direct me now rather than using my consciousness to feel positive and design my ideal reality."*

One does not suddenly "feel motivated" any more than one suddenly and without cause feels happy. Happiness is a result of thought, not impulse. It is our mind's reasoning that what we are experiencing in the moment (or in life in general) is pleasurable, positive, and appreciated. An enduring sense of happiness is a prolonged intellectual high that comes from positive memory and choice, not a temporary physical pleasure.

And so mature adults realize that motivation is not an accident, *not so much a feeling* as it is a conscious commitment to a motive, a choice toward something, *a deeply held reason to act.* It is an energy that results from thought. We feel motivated because we choose to, not because the sun happens to shine on our side of the street.

> *So if we want more motivation in our lives, we must make clearer choices and more deeply commit to them.*

Can it be so simple? All we do is make clear choices and deeply commit to making them happen and we feel motivated? Yes, to some degree. But mastery comes in understanding the nuances of this effort. There is a process that we can follow to more consciously activate and amplify motivation. Gaining command of this process gives us the intellectual and emotional ability to summon motivation to any degree we desire, for any length, and at any time we choose.

SPARKING MOTIVATION

Psychologically, motivation is sparked by the energy created by *ambition* and *expectancy*. Ambition is the *choice* to be, have, do, or experience something *greater* in our lives.

As soon as we want something greater for ourselves, our motivation is sparked. Do we want a better job? A better home? A better marriage? A better body? A better life? From such desires our energies are aroused; the higher the desire, the higher the initial sense of motivation we feel.

So we must go within and ask: "What do I want for myself? What new goal would be meaningful to me? What am I excited about learning or giving? What great new adventure do I dream of? What grand pursuit or act of service will be satisfying to me and get me out of the bed each morning?" Such questions are the secret to stoking ambition, and thus motivation.

It's simple:

> *By deeply contemplating higher aims,*
> *we energize ourselves to pursue them.*

There is more. Many people want something better for themselves—their ambition *is* alive and well—but they still do not feel motivated. Why? Because despite the hope for something more, they don't *believe it can happen,* or that *they* can make it happen. They lack *expectancy*—a choice to believe that their dreams are possible and that they can achieve them. Imagine the aspiring actor who never auditions—she *wants* to be an actor but does not believe in her ability to make it happen. Consider the would-be entrepreneur, who wants to start a business but never leaves his job because he doesn't believe he can make it on his own. These people learn a tough life truth: Desire without belief in self is ultimately deflating.

Often, when motivation is lacking, we don't truly *expect* that we will realize our aim. And if we don't believe it, we know we cannot achieve it, so we won't even try. In this way, *expectancy is the great differentiator between mere hope and motivation.* When we find ourselves hopeful but not motivated, we need to add a little more faith to the mix, to tell ourselves, "I expect that it will happen no matter what, because I have faith in myself to learn and grow and, day by day, make things happen. I will make my dreams a reality over time because I trust my ability to learn, to work, to ask for help, to persist." With these expectations, our minds begin to form the beliefs and behaviors needed to make our ambitions a reality.

So let us focus our minds on seeing our dreams come true, and on seeing ourselves make it happen. Let us sit down tonight and think of what more would bring joy and fulfillment into our lives. Let us journal about it and dream about it. Let us imagine ourselves doing great things with boldness and fire and commitment. This is visualization and internalization—a process of weaving expectancy deep into our psyche and the fabric of our being. This is the process of sparking our own motivation.

Consider the man who wants to compete in a triathlon. In order to succeed, he knows he cannot say to himself, "I hope one day that I get in good enough shape to maybe do a triathlon." Instead, he clarifies why he has this ambition, and he tells himself that he will race to the best of his ability and succeed; he visualizes himself in the water, on the bike, on the run, crossing the finish line. He summons up his motivation and makes the choice to begin, to train, to succeed—because he believes he *must* and he believes he *can.*

So, to those who say, "I wish I were more motivated," we reply, "Do not hope for motivation; choose an ambition to become motivated for. Fix on a dream and believe that it will see daylight and soon a great swell of enthusiasm will enliven you."

SUSTAINING MOTIVATION

Ambition and expectation are just the beginning of the process. They are the *spark* of motivation. Unfortunately, many people never fan the flames of motivation by keeping their focus on their dreams. The triathlete must do more than simply believe in his dream once in a while. He must continue making choices that *sustain* the desire. He must schedule his routines. He must get a coach. He must run and sweat and fight for growth. And he must do this over and over again.

The sustaining choices of motivation are thus *attention* and *effort*.

Motivation feels fickle only to those who have been inattentive to their ambitions. An undirected mind has little drive other than the baseline human impulses, sustained motivation *not* being among them. We must refocus. Giving our ambitions consistent mental attention keeps the drive alive, our energies swirling in anticipation. This can be as easy as reviewing our goals each day, journaling about our desires each night, regularly setting aside moments to visualize what we want and schedule our next steps.

This is where so many people fail. The distractions of the day steal their mental focus and thus their motivation. The real downfall for many people isn't that they are "unmotivated" people, but that they are simply *distracted*, too absentminded to sustain motivation. It may be that the world isn't giving us what we want simply because our own lack of focus makes it unclear what we are asking for.

We mustn't let our dreams die in the daylight because we lose focus while responding to the world's lame interests or false emergencies.

We mustn't take our eyes off our own goals, as we dispatch mundane tasks of the day or await the "right time" to begin what we truly want to do. When we allow our attention to drift from our dreams and into the vast sea of unawareness, our motivation is dragged along behind it.

So let us keep our minds on our motives. Let us hold our grand visions in view, with dreams popping with color across the conscious dashboard of our minds every single day. Let us sit and meditate on what we want and see those desires come into fruition over and over again.

Some might fear that we are cultivating an obsession. We are. We are becoming obsessed with a mighty aim, putting our full attention and zeal, perhaps for the first time, into something that truly *matters* to us. We should not fear an obsession for building a great and free life. Without such willed attention, our motivation would descend into halfhearted hopes, flirty arousals of the heart that have no staying power.

It is the obvious equation and the ultimate secret:
the deeper and longer I give attention to my ambitions and passions,
the more motivation I feel.

But we cannot merely *think* our way to sustained motivation; we must *work* our way toward it. We must put *real effort* into reaching our ambitions. We cannot attract or have that which we do not *act* toward. Is it not true that we can easily discern the depth of a person's motivation by observing how consistently they have been taking action toward their dreams? The less consistent someone's effort, the more obvious it is that they lack motivation. The irony is that if they gave more *effort*, they would have more *motivation*.

We cannot feel sustained energy or commitment for completing a journey if we have never taken the first step. The triathlete must have ambition but he must also begin to *train*. He must sign up for the race, begin running farther, train harder, stretch his comfort zones, *work* for his dream of crossing that finish line. From those efforts, his motivation will be sustained and enlarged.

When motivation dies, then it's not because our dreams died; it's because we never began—or didn't sustain—any real *effort*. Without taking steps forward, we never sense the highs of progress and soon the energy is gone and, almost predictably, we quit.

We often forget that it is sweat and toil toward meaningful pursuits that makes us truly alive. So let us remember that nothing keeps motivation aflame more than hard work and the resulting momentum and fulfillment. To continue our efforts toward our ambitions *despite* fatigue and distraction and hardship—*this* is the mark of the truly motivated.

Our life and legend hinge on our ability to keep marching on, to keep firing our will over the long term. Just one more heavy step toward our dreams often awakens the desire to follow it with another. And so the answer becomes clear when people ask, "What is the ultimate secret to life-long motivation?" *Continuing on—no matter what.*

It hurts to think that, after all of our struggles to feel more motivated, all we needed to do was give more attention to our ambitions. We would rather believe that during those roaring times of our lives when we were fired up, there was luck or an external force at play. We want to fall for the fallacy that we were more motivated because of environmental factors: our back was against the wall, our dad died, our wife needed us, the big door of opportunity swung open, God touched us, there was a baby to feed.

But the stark reality is that those times we were motivated happened simply because we were *willing* and *working* ourselves forward more often. There was attention. There was effort. These things were daily, relentless, and inextinguishable. And these things were choices—we *chose* to give more attention and more effort toward something meaningful. There was no more. *Choice* energized us; *it* was our savior, not the grace of changing circumstance or dire need or even divine calling—for how many people have heard such a call but chose not to respond? It is in choosing to respond to circumstances or need or God in our own way, as a free and driven person, and with real action, that we emerge from the darkness.

Let it be clear to all: Greatness belongs to those who have mastered the ability to focus relentlessly on their ambitions and act decisively toward them.

AMPLIFYING MOTIVATION

We have aroused our motivation and we have kept it burning. Now let us grow it and condition it through every fiber of our being and into every facet of our lives. Two choices will amplify our motivation to another level: *attitude* and *environment*.

Attitude matters. Free and motivated people are *positive* and *enthusiastic* about their goals and their lives. Yet look at the millions of people drowning in the quicksand of pessimism, gritting their teeth in contempt at their everyday experiences. Anger, hatred, and all the trappings of fear fuel the minds of the masses. There is a dispirited gloom hanging over so many. But why? Is there a sudden reason to feel profoundly more negative about life? No. The issue at hand is a failure to *choose* one's attitude. Most people rarely even *think* about their disposition or how they are energetically experiencing or contributing to the world. This inattention to how they think and behave and serve—this *unconscious style*—is costing them their dreams and legacy. Just think of the people who have achieved great things. Are they sullen and bitter? Negative and angry? No. What person ever achieved true greatness and fulfillment with a universally bad attitude? Those with a miserable attitude rarely move the needle of the world toward progress.

Motivation never kindles anyone's soul to its brightest burn unless he or she is open-minded and fired with an enthusiasm for life. An open and positive disposition toward the world can attract people, bring joy into our experience, and channel the highest energies of the universe. So let us remember that in all circumstances, we can choose how we show up and feel and relate with the world. We must make it a game to meet difficult circumstances with a smile, good-natured intent, humor, and a cheering voice that rises above the somber murmurs of the aimless crowd. Keeping one's attitude positive, especially when the world conspires to make us mad, is one of the great accomplishments of life.

Outside of our direct will, one way to keep ourselves sane and positive is to surround ourselves with people who are sane and positive.

Few things amplify our long-term motivation
more than a positive social environment.

Whom we interact with matters to our attitude, and thus to our motivation.

Unfortunately, most people have allowed their motivation to be dampened by the social spheres to which they restrict themselves. It is hard, though not impossible, to be highly motivated when surrounded by pessimists and jerks, or while living in the stress and chaos created by the drama queens and the absentminded. It is also the rare individual who spends his days couch surfing and partying with drunken friends, then ends up stumbling on the secret to success and happiness. The woman with the demeaning boyfriend rarely feels motivated to be her best self, and the man working a dead-end job with an insulting boss and bored coworkers rarely feels motivated to contribute with excellence.

For once and for all, we should distance ourselves from those with bad attitudes, for their energy is contagious and corrupting. We should remember our Personal Freedom is on the line, and so our social sphere mustn't hinder our self-expression or pursuit of things that are meaningful.

For motivation's sake, we must be vigilant and surround ourselves with genuine and positive people who seek positive aims with positive attitudes.

Let us also be more disciplined in shaping our *physical environments* to amplify our emotions. We should *love* the spaces we spend our time in, and if we do not, we should make immediate changes. Walking into our homes should bring peace and the ability to rejuvenate. We should have plenty of light and a place where we cannot be disturbed so that we can reflect, think, plan, make art. We should feel comfortable where we sleep and where we think. Our workspaces should inspire us. And we should have a ready contact list of other driven people to call upon when we need new inspiration. If we do not, again we must make immediate changes to find and cultivate such relationships. If we lack a supportive place to live and work, or a positive peer group, let it be our mission to manifest those things in our lives. Our environment matters and so we shall shape it to lift us into the next realm of motivation and joy.

A CLEAR PATH FROM VICTIMHOOD

With this new understanding of our motivation, we move away from victimhood and find a clear path toward freedom. We can now bring motivation to life at any moment, and we can tell others how to do it:

Choose an ambition and, with full force,
expect that it is possible and that you can make it happen.
Give constant attention and committed effort to your dreams,
and your motivation will perpetuate itself.
Demonstrate a positive attitude as you strive
for great things and take care to create a supportive
environment around you that amplifies your motivation.

With such practices, cultivating motivation moves from a lucky feeling to a *willed choice.* Over time, these choices will lead us to feel in command of our lives, able to punch through distractions, and better at riding the ups and downs of existence. Without such practices, we fall whim to our impulses and slave to laziness and fear. We fall victim to others and to circumstances because we cannot rouse ourselves to be mindful or break free. Soon we are unmotivated victims, and nothing deadens the energies of the soul like a sense of victimhood.

And so we have a message to the aimless and the unmotivated:

They say, "I am waiting for something or someone to motivate me."

We say: Motivation is summoned only from within.

They say, "I do not feel motivated; I'm just not a motivated person."

We say: Motivation is not an impulse of the body or a personality trait; it is an intention and will of a free and conscious mind.

They say, "I'll get more motivation and work harder when my job gives me more pay, autonomy, and responsibility."

We say: If you have not chosen to be motivated before, that is why you do not have more pay, autonomy, and responsibility. Effort gives you motivation, and motivation gives you reward.

They say, "The people around me keep killing my motivation."

We say: You are choosing the people around you, but, regardless, motivation is of your own will and volition—it is imperishable and cannot be granted, diminished, or killed by others. It exists within you because you want it to. The birth, life, and death of each day's motivation are subject to your own direction.

They say, "Well, I haven't had any major life experiences that have motivated me, like a lucky break or a life event that made me find my purpose."

We say: Purpose does not strike as a lucky lightning bolt of inspiration. Motivation and purpose are choices. The only thing needed to spark motivation is a decision to heighten your ambition and expectancy—to sit down, think about what you desire, and believe you can go get it. To keep that motivation, you must give constant attention and effort.

They say, "Sometimes I just feel lazy."

We say: Then choose to feel something else. Laziness is a choice just as any other feeling can be a choice. Understand that life is short, and that choosing laziness for the long-term will lead to a life that is slave to impulse and littered with regrets. Only in choosing to energize yourself will you finally go out into the world, discover who you are, grow, actualize your dreams, and become free and great.

LIFE ENLARGED AND GLORIFIED

To be aware, to utilize our full mental faculties as humans, to be directors of our own minds and motives—*these things* give us personal power. Let us never neglect them, and let us devote ourselves to mastering motivation each day of our lives. There is nothing so deserving of our vital attention, for it is in the millions of in-the-moment decisions made throughout our lives—either directed by a motivated mind that bends toward Personal Freedom or left to the default impulses that bend toward fear—that we create our destiny. Fear wins or freedom wins.

Life is enlarged and glorified when motivation is alight. So let us once more spark our souls with an ambitious fire. Let us stoke this energy with close attention, constant effort, and positive attitude. Let us act with full efficacy in shaping the social and physical environments of our lives. Should we be diligent and should we succeed, our vitality will amplify, our life will magnify as if a divine light is bursting through, signaling to the world and to destiny that we are here, that it is our time, that we are *ready*.

SECTION TWO

THE 9 DECLARATIONS

———

DECLARATION I

WE SHALL MEET LIFE WITH FULL PRESENCE AND POWER

---•---

Your true home is in the here and the now.

THÍCH NHAT HANH

A N AFFLICTION IS STEALING JOY FROM THE WORLD'S people, poisoning what was meant to be a divinely inspired experience of freedom. It is a haunting absence from the present moment.

Too many have checked out of their bodies and their lives. They are not attuned to the energy and circumstances around them, nor do they understand their responsibilities to those things in this very moment. They have little awe or reverence for the blessings around them, acting as if they preferred to be somewhere else, as if they were mentally living in distant time zones, hours behind or ahead of the joyous tick and bliss of Now. Their life force thus seems detached and dissipated, their lives unaccounted for and unlived, their souls a world away.

The majority of humanity seems lost in the abyss of unawareness. The hollow and glazed eyes of so many reveal it all: minds trapped in the dark, unfeeling hinterlands of distraction and thoughtlessness. They are not sleeping but they are not conscious, alert, purposeful. They are buzzed out on coffee but without awareness there is no real center of energy, no grounding, no vibrant feel for the Now.

Life is not meant to be a long series of unfelt and undirected experiences. We are not to be zombies and slaves, unconscious animals trapped in dumbness to the moment, leading mindless and powerless lives. We are not intended to be inattentive to our loved ones and the duties of life or the dreams in our hearts.

Should we wish to be free and alive with full power, we must decide to bring the full might of our conscious mind to the present experience. We must choose to *feel* again. We must *sense* this life.

Let us remember that *all that we love of life can be accessed only now.* All we seek is here, with us and available to us in this moment. All the real riches—love, passion, joy, satisfaction, harmony—are available *now* on the menu of the mind, available for us to savor should we awake and order them. All that we seek to become is also here; we can choose what role we want to play and how we will direct life's energies in each moment. Should we learn to direct our awareness and power in all we do, then discontent shall disappear and a vital energy will return. We will sense a vibrancy unfathomable to most men and women of this Earth. For this, let us declare: *We Shall Meet Life with Full Presence and Power.*

THE HALF-EXPERIENCED LIFE

So much of our lives goes unnoticed. We miss the sunrises and sunsets. We don't sense how we're feeling for hours and often days at a time. We didn't see the kind stranger help the elderly man cross the street. We missed that appreciative smile on our spouse's face. We didn't sense our coworker's desperation because we never paused to look her in the eye or ask about her day. Locked indoors and hidden behind machines, we missed the entire season—the winter passed and we didn't play in the snow, the spring bloomed and we overlooked the flowers, the summer and the fall passed so quickly and we don't even remember the trees changing or feel satisfied with the time we spent outside. Each day there are a million divine wonders, acts of human kindness, and beautiful sights. Yet we are too checked out or busy thinking about yesterday or tomorrow to even sense the magic.

We mustn't be so numb or absentminded as to allow ourselves to suffer the fate and misery of those choosing a half-interested, half-engaged life. We mustn't stay oblivious to the key moments and circumstances of our lives. There is more pulse and beauty and meaning to be had.

With enlightenment comes the realization
that the natural foe to life is not a distant death,
but a detachment from living.

Reality is only here, now, and we must learn to face it, feel it, and form it.

The present is all there is. Motivation, and life itself, cannot be sensed separate from Now. Without bringing our full consciousness to the moment, we became slave to impulse or tired inclination, subservient to our base conditioning that tends to lean toward ease and fear rather than growth and freedom. From this space of disengagement emerges all that we disdain: the barely present parent, the halfhearted lover, the unfocused student, the absent leader.

It is time to become more alert and engaged in the world. As the next moments of our lives unfold, we can choose to pay more attention to how we feel, to how others feel, to the blessings all around. We can give others the full beam of our focus and affection. We can open our hearts, minds, and spirits to what the universe whispers to us. We can choose once more to be in this very moment, open and free—*alive.*

Our only enemy in this effort is ourselves. To gain greater presence, we will need to overcome our habit of living in the past or future. And we will need to become more aware of the roles and responsibilities we can choose each and every moment as free, conscious, and motivated people.

RIPPED FROM TIME

The reason most of us lack vitality is that we are unconsciously or obsessively directing our minds to the past or future at the expense of fully living now. Life cannot be sensed a day before or a day ahead. We must learn to release our habits of nostalgia and absurd projection and reenter our lives in the moment.

We begin by releasing the past. There is very little use in thinking about yesterday or the days before it. Unless recounting its joys or looking for its lessons that may help us Now, it is best to release the past entirely. All else comes at a dire effect to our joy and freedom in the moment.

This work is difficult. Most people have become addicted to obsessing about their past, either wishing for its return or blaming it for frustration in their lives today. The cost is that they cannot be spontaneous—they are acting from an identity that is but a glorified or terrorized mental reflection. Spontaneity is the hallmark of a free person, and no person stuck thinking about yesterday—positively or negatively—can be truly liberated in the moment.

Some will say, "But I *liked* yesterday more than today. I'd rather focus on the glory days and remember who I was than face who I am today." This is the statement of a person who has resigned their personal power. *They have become a collection of walking memories rather than a mission-driven human.* They are now weak-willed and unambitious, wasted in a perpetual memory that prevents their real life from progressing. Life will continue to be a reminiscent myth unless they discover that their only path out of the past lies in the very day before them. What will bring motivation and glory to their lives once more is a new mental discipline of bringing their focus back to the moment, in being authentic and *active* today. Without such conscious ambition and attention, only a negative circumstance can right them—a catastrophe or severe need might pop them from the past and help them refocus on Now.

We should hope such jarring will be unnecessary and they will simply choose to reengage with their current life because it will make them happy and alive once more.

If we revisit the past for brief and joyous recollections, let us be sure to take note of what exactly made us happy. We will see that happiness came from those moments in which we were vitally *aware*. Something was happening, and we noticed it with awe or appreciation—there was beauty, surprise, pleasure, passion, fun, love, and peace, perhaps all of these in a glorious span of moments. The world came into sharp focus for an instant. Meaningless things faded away and meaningful things enlarged and drew our eye. There was authenticity and freshness to the experience. There was oneness with the moment. We became alert and connected to something positive, and that is why we can so easily recall it.

Good memories can be celebrated. But let us not forget that, even in the house of happiness, a positive past can become an unwanted guest preventing us from the day's activities and freedom. Even though we have these positive associations, let us not drift too long in our minds at the cost of missing those very things that are accessible to us right here and now. What made us happy was awareness of the moment. Let us not forget that. Let us use this knowledge as a life practice and come back to Now with full vibrancy.

Others think of the past and say, "But I *hate* the past. It is the cause of all my problems today." They direct obsessive energies to looking backward with a sneer and a pointed finger. They would rather not think of the past and yet they do, because they have mentally tied the thick rope of resentment around old situations. Despite time and the changing world, they are still bitter about an old upset, frightful of an old fear, victim to an old situation. They are now the angry person, the whining victim, or the regretful philosopher.

It is very easy to become one of these people because our past has shaped us so much. But we must not. Any dirt or carnage of yesterday belongs nowhere near Now but rather in the dustbin of history, where we need not rummage about. Dwelling on past injuries only leaves us dispirited and torn from the moment.

If yesterday's hardships are stealing our aliveness today, then we must seek another level of consciousness. For some, this will require therapy to work through. For most, it will at the very least require diligence in immediately releasing negative thoughts and instead choosing to ask, "What can I focus on in my life at this exact moment to sense some peace, appreciation, or enthusiasm? What kind of person and what kind of experience do I want to choose to manifest *right now?*" To those who have such presence of mind belong a life that is connected, real, and positive.

Forgetting Tomorrow

Many people are checked out of today because they are thinking about tomorrow.

For some, there is a secret fear that tomorrow will be worse than today. They lie awake stewing on the hardships that tomorrow might bring. Their fears about the future rip them from the blessings of the moment.

Others are concerned that tomorrow won't be worse but rather no different at all. They think, "Why can't my life be more exciting? Tomorrow is just going to be another day, another dollar. Just another replay of the same old routine." The sad reality is that, unless they learn to grip their present experience with a renewed fervor, they are correct.

Still others look to the future in a different way—they are the daydreamers lost in positive musings about what is possible for them. They often sit at their desk and let their minds drift into visions of tomorrow, and nothing brings them back but a phone call or knock at the door. Tragically their feet rarely land in Now. They are always wishing on a star, but not working here on earth to enjoy their experience or progress their lives.

Just like with the past, there is nothing wrong with journeying into the future if it brings joy or instruction. But that journey must be brief and never come at the expense of owning the hour. Plan and dream when those things are called for, yes, but don't disconnect from the magic and tasks and people at hand.

A better future can be imagined for segments of time,
but it is only in this time that a better future can be built.

Regardless of their memories or dreams for tomorrow, the masters of this life are always bringing their focus back to this very moment. They live serenely in the Now, benefiting from yesterday without yearning for it, hopeful for tomorrow but not obsessing over it. They are vigilant in directing their attentions and affections to their immediate circumstances and people surrounding them. They frequently ask themselves, "Is my mind alert now? Am I noticing and fully sensing what is around me, and taking it all in? Am I *feeling* this life? Am I directing my full power to what is in front of me and what matters?"

AVOIDING REALITY

Some among us haven't the strength to ask such questions, preferring the easy escape from life that is avoidance. They prefer to turn away from the responsibilities or circumstances right in front of them. They remove themselves mentally, emotionally, and spiritually from Now, since engaging would involve hardship and unflinching self-examination. This is the man who avoids listening to his wife's requests because it will require him to remove himself from the couch, the leader who avoids the meeting because she would have to face the fact her business is failing, the student who goes out on the town rather than completing a difficult assignment, the man with the medical condition who refuses to go to the hospital because it might mean something is very wrong with his body and death is drawing near.

To the immature or unconscious person, it feels sane to avoid the hardships that life thrusts at them. It makes sense to remove their attention from circumstances that bring discomfort. It's easier to stop doing the hard task right in front of them, to disperse their attention onto multiple easier tasks. It is tempting to check out, to run and hide. But in doing so, we avoid life itself. The casualty is our own presence and power. When we lack the courage or discipline to address what we must, our presence is never wielded and honed, and so life becomes devoid of feeling and happiness. Avoidance may be the best short-term strategy to avoid pain and conflict, but it is also the best long-term strategy to ensure suffering.

All things must be dealt with and Now is the time to begin. If a difficult conversation awaits with one's spouse, then the conversation should be had this day. If the business is in peril, then do not go on vacation or miss the meeting; get to work fixing the issue at hand. If the paper is due, begin writing. If the body is sick, go to the doctor. Any other action is avoidance, and where there is avoidance there can ultimately be no peace or progress.

Free and motivated people do not neglect reality.

They meet difficulty with attention, seeing these as opportunities to test their faith, strength, and love. Knowing that life is full of strife, but trusting in themselves and their path, they seek to handle whatever life demands of them directly and swiftly. Through practice, they learn to find comfort in the uncomfortable, and true mastery in life. We can learn from them. Let us never look hardship in the face and run. To do so is to tear ourselves from this world and this time, and to relinquish our growth and contributions in life. Let us always remember that in addressing our pain and fear, we gain mastery over them. In meeting challenge rather than avoiding it, we find success. In meeting Fate's well-placed opportunities for growth, we become favored. And so let us ask ourselves, "What should I finally face in my life? What truths or realities are preventing my growth and happiness? What could I do about it right now? How can I better connect with this moment so that I can master what the hour demands of me?"

INATTENTION TO OUR ROLES

Being fully present in life not only means being observant and unfailing in addressing our realities, but also deciding to proactively *choose* our roles and behaviors each day.

In any given moment, we can play one or a combination of five vital roles. Inattention to these possible roles leads to a life without intention. But bringing our awareness to them helps us activate our full personal power in each moment. It brings purpose to our minds and activities. And *purpose* is the greatest bridge to Now.

Observer

The first role we can play in our lives is *observer*, or the conscious viewer. This is the role and responsibility we are charged with through the gift of self-awareness. As observer, we can float above our reality and view the totality of who we are in life and the minutia of how we are acting and reacting in the very moment. It is not a detachment from ourselves or the moment, but rather a careful observance of it.

Those who have mastered this role can make a decision and almost simultaneously evaluate whether or not it is the *right* decision. They can sense themselves doing, feeling, and thinking things, and know if those things are authentic. They notice when they are making poor decisions, being rude to others, forgetting something important. They are vitally aware of themselves. They can sense a conflict brewing and feel their anger lifting yet choose not to act on that anger. It is as though they have an internal dialogue: "Oh, I see that I am becoming upset about this situation. Why am I reacting this way right now? Will anger serve me in this moment? If I were responding as my highest self, what would I say and do right now?"

We can learn to master this role by practicing self-examination. Several times throughout the day, we can ask ourselves, "If I stopped and hovered above my life, what do I see myself doing, and why do I think I am doing that? Why am I feeling what I am feeling right now? What result will happen from my current actions and intentions? What is it I can sense that my mind, body, and spirit truly feel and need and desire right now?" When we grasp this idea of sensing ourselves, we become more connected to ourselves and our lives. This must be our goal.

Director

The second role is the more proactive role as *director*, the conscious and intentional creator of our lives. If we can imagine life as a movie, then we can imagine ourselves as the one directing each scene and character within it. The director calls all the shots and is the ultimate planner and authority on what each character is doing, why they are doing it, and what they are going to do next. The director chooses where to focus the camera in each second of filming. The director makes well-reasoned choices about the characters in order to shape a compelling and meaningful story.

From this simple metaphor we can draw much wisdom for improving our lives. Those who are unhappy with the current story of their life are those who have not been directing its scenes and characters. They lacked a plan for their story. They wandered in and out of situations in their lives without any real intent. They focused on the wrong things, often zooming in on the negative aspects of life while missing the beautiful or interesting. They let the wrong characters enter the important scenes. They rarely stepped back from the frame to see the big picture. They let themselves respond to situations not as a noble and heroic character but as a whiny child screeching across the stage of life.

Mastering the role of the director requires us to be detailed in our intentions for each scene in our story. If we are going out on a date with our spouse this evening, how do we want the scene to unfold? What kind of person do we want to be at the dinner table? How will we appear and what will we sound like? How will we respond to her descriptions of her day? What surprises will keep the scene fresh? How might the entire evening be a romantic love affair captured through our own eyes? Where is this story with this person going to go?

Playing the director of our own movie gives us the ability to choose our entire character and life's arc. Will our character be strong or weak, noble or selfish, stressed or peaceful, flighty or grounded? Will each of our days say something about who we are, and if so, what? What will we demonstrate

and become in the next scene of our lives? These are important questions. If we do not ask them, we fail to focus on the
story of our lives and thus we become lost within it. Worse,
we become bit players in *other* people's stories, casualties of the
larger mass narrative that is a boring tale of conformity. So let
us be more conscious: *What shall our life's story be and how can
we direct our thoughts and actions to make that vision a reality?*

Guardian

The third role deserving our attention is that of *guardian*
to our mind, body, and soul. We must stand at the gates
of our life and protect ourselves from unwanted contami-
nants: negative information, people, and habits.

How often we fail in this role. We let such useless
information, tripe, and stupidity into our minds. We
dumbly consume words, images, and sounds from salacious
sources that masquerade their alerts and offers as somehow
relevant to our lives. This is the news media that pretends
some ignorant and extremist view might enlighten us, the
network that says the reality of a few entitled brats being
filmed without filter might entertain us, the webpage that
cons us into thinking we are miserable without their prod-
uct. From all this we do not grow wiser but less informed,
not entertained but numbed, not wealthier but poorer.

Everything we consume becomes a part of us. All the
useless factoids and scandals do nothing but take root in our
psyche and emerge as stupidity and drama later on. Seeing
people being petty on television a million times makes us
pettier. As guardian of our mind, we mustn't allow the trite

and negative to enter so easily. We should be conscious of the information entering our minds. If we set out to learn something, let us be purposeful about the source, seeking to feed our brain with positive, empowering information that moves our lives forward. If we want to be entertained, let us choose the form of entertainment that would truly enliven us—that would bring a depth of understanding or appreciation into our lives. In all cases, let us remain at our post as the protector of a healthy and vital mind. What we see and hear and allow into our brains shapes our personality and our destiny.

We must also be guardians of our bodies. The plight of those in abundance cultures brimming with fake food is that convenience thwarts common sense. Rather than choosing food that is real, whole, and good for us, we choose what is fast and sweet. As a society, we have become not guardians but gorgers, stuffing and poisoning ourselves, mindlessly toxifying the very structure that houses our heart and soul.

Most people would feel guilty
for destroying someone else's property.
Yet they wreck the very temple their Creator gifted them.

It is time we protect our health by paying more attention to what we are putting in our mouths. There is no lack of information on how to choose a healthy diet or live a healthier lifestyle. Eat smaller portions. Make a plate of mostly whole foods and greens. Limit consumption of processed food or anything with unpronounceable ingredients. Stop eating so much sugar. Move more, and exercise several times per week to maintain a healthy, strong body. Drink more water and get more sleep. None of this is new information. What is required is a new *commitment* to caring for our bodies. If we let the energy of our body fade, our motivation soon goes with it.

Let us be equally vigilant in evaluating the people we let into our lives. Are we allowing tyrants, jackals, and jerks to contaminate our environment? Who are the negative people poisoning our potential and why are they in our space? Are we constantly allowing ourselves to be hurt? Are we surrounding ourselves by whiners and haters? To one and all: *They must go.* And we mustn't hope that they will go—they will loiter as long as we allow. It is up to us to be fierce guardians of our happiness and humanity in life. This often requires direct communication, to tell others to leave, to adjust their attitude, to be kinder and more supportive. It requires being more assertive and demanding. No one likes to do this kind of work. But we must protect ourselves from sour humans. By the same token, we must surround ourselves with positive, kind, and inspiring people. We can choose to call to them from the gates of our lives, inviting them into our circles and homes, asking them to share their insights and lives with us.

Warrior

The next role is the *warrior.* Should we sit in our homes and find life wanting, then we must stand and venture out to fight purposefully for something more. We must be bold, fierce, and unrelenting in chasing our dreams. We must push aside our fears, struggle with conviction, battle through all obstacles. We must want to win, to bring back treasures and glory to our homes, to leave nothing on the battlefields of life but the legend of our courage and might.

We will have made nothing of ourselves or created anything significant unless we prepare for the long and arduous journey to mastery. What skills must we have to win our next battles? Let us acquire them now. What tools and resources will we need? Let us ready them now. Who will we need to march with us so that we can have camaraderie and support in taking the next mountain? Let us seek to meet and enlist them now. What must we sacrifice in order to ascend even higher? Let us sacrifice it now before it weighs us down on the journey.

Owning the role of warrior requires us to take stock of all the things we are deeply committed to in life. The warrior asks, "What will I stand for in life? How will I bring honor and abundance to my loved ones? What adventures will make me feel alive? What do I want and how hard am I prepared to fight for it?"

This matter of hard work reveals whether we are the cowards or warriors of this world. Perhaps it is time we step back from all our busywork and think again about our greater dreams and glory. Let us be honest and brave in assessing our lives, asking, "How *hard* am I really working toward my dream? Am I letting little obstacles stop my progress, or am I battling through them on a consistent basis? Am I doing what I must to prepare my mind, body, and soul for victory? Am I acting with real conviction and commitment in life, or simply trudging through? Have

I struggled to succeed in any area of my life because I've failed to sacrifice or commit?"

If we have real dreams, then we must fight for them. For the sake of our soul and our families, we must adopt that warrior spirit that is hungry, ambitious, and courageous.

The essence of the warrior spirit is *readiness*—a bias toward action.

Warriors do not waste time in making decisions. There is little hesitation, hemming, hawing, or hedging. Warriors do not await perfect circumstances to begin the long march to victory; they do not stop when tired or frightened; they do not shy away from a needed fight; they do not apologize for boldness or strength.

No, when there is a conquest, when they see fortune in lands on the horizon, they set out, they march, they march, and they march. On their path, they have gravity about them, a seriousness, a commitment, a strong center. They are solid no matter how much turmoil and uncertainty lurks beneath. Their fire, will, and discipline are uncommon, sometimes causing others to fear their ambition, and yet always they earn respect for their courage. "There they go," the watchers on the sidelines of life say. "That person is a *fighter* and will not give up."

So what is it that we are fighting for? To real warriors, this is a burning question, something deeply contemplated. Warriors take pride and dignity from their answers to such a question. Their commitments are important to them, and every small victory toward those commitments is logged, celebrated, integrated into their identity, shared joyously with their tribe of fellow strivers. They are fully aware of the fact they are warriors and creating a warrior ethos, a legend as a fighter for things both important to themselves and also grander and more significant than themselves. *They are giving their lives to something that matters.*

To become stronger warriors, we must stop all the hesitations and excuses. We must commit to fighting harder and longer toward our dreams. So let us write down all the things we've been waiting to do, along with all our excuses for not doing them. Let us contemplate where we are being weak in our lives or progressing too slowly. Then let us get recommitted and decide that tomorrow, no matter what, we will march with courage toward our dreams regardless of the obstacles in our way. Let us be obsessive and fierce about our progress once more. Warriors are stubborn and strict, clear about what they fight for and committed to every discipline required to win the next battle. For the fate of our dreams and for the security and abundance of our families, let our character be so solid.

Lover

While on our quests, we must never forget *whom* we are fighting for. There are people we care for and who need us. No victory is sweet and no life fulfilling without someone to celebrate with and care for. And so let us master our role as *lover.*

Lovers have a stunning capacity for shining attention and adoration on others. They take a vital interest in others so that they may understand them, care for them, and contribute meaningfully to their lives. They communicate from the heart and seek to enlarge the heart of those around them by giving them respect and empathy.

This may be the most difficult role and responsibility to master. Our relationships demand *more* presence, *more* attention, and *more* purposeful tending than any other area of our lives, yet how often we cause our own disappointment, heartbreak, and separation. Think of all the wrecked relationships that could have been saved with just a few more minutes' worth of time, attention, and affection. Witness the father yell at his daughter without regard for her feelings or needs. Observe the wife at the table, staring at her phone rather than conversing with her spouse. Recall the time a loved one needed a kind word but we were too busy. All the darkness and sadness caused in these situations would be preventable if there were a higher focus on love.

In a modern world plagued by distraction, our greatest work in becoming better lovers is in reconnecting with those who have already given us their hearts. We have to finally stop all the looking about and once more peer into the eyes of those we adore. We have to ask them more questions. How was their day, *really?* What are they struggling with? What would make them feel more alive and happy? How can we connect with and care for them better? *Is there a way we can demonstrate even more affection and appreciation for them?*

We must learn to sit down each day and think about the health and growth of our loved ones as much as we think about the growth of our careers. Are there rituals we can create to bring us all closer? To rekindle the fire and passion? To move our lives forward, together?

Each of us was fashioned from love. Our nature is love, and our hearts beat with it and our spirit soars with its quickening power. Let us reconnect with our hearts and the hearts of others. Let us embody this role with such vitality and power that in the bright beams of our love those around us are stunned and overjoyed and honored and enlivened.

Leader

There are men and women counting on us and looking to our example. They await our direction and action. We owe it to them to be outstanding in our role as *leader*.

The world is in dire need of leaders. Because we lack them, so many individuals and institutions are barreling blindly in the dark. Society is not being moored to the demands of good character and the expectations to serve the common good. And so the world is intoxicated by greed, mad passions, and intolerance. Without leaders at the helm of humanity, what should be a joyous collective ride toward hope, freedom, and abundance for all is instead a terrible, directionless drive with spoiled brats too ignorant and proud to ask for directions, a careening vehicle headed to catastrophe.

We must begin again the great work of uplifting humankind.

Our times demand vision and disciplined, collaborative effort to make a real difference. These things are inspired and sustained by good leaders. And so let us ask ourselves, "What can be done to improve this world that I influence? How can I help others solve problems and achieve their dreams? Who can I enlist and empower to help achieve something remarkable? How can I unlock the potential of those around me to do more good?"

Perhaps if more people asked these kinds of questions, we could stop society's headlong drive into oblivion. Yet some of us fear taking a leadership role. But what is our excuse? In the final reckoning of our life's legacy, shall we explain to our Creator that He did not equip us well enough for the task? No. We must forget the excuses and remember our duty to serve something larger than ourselves.

Look back at history. When good decisions and progress were made at the important crossroads of each era, there were always bold and motivated people with clear vision and sure voices. Let us be *that* for our generation. The call for leadership is all around. Let's not play deaf to the needs of the world at this moment of crisis. There are things to volunteer for and lead in our neighborhoods and communities. There are untapped sources of potential and power in our businesses. And so let us decide now to do our best to spot those areas of need, to lift those around us, to unite people in meaningful struggle and service once more. For the betterment of our world, it is time to take charge once more.

THE MOMENT NOW

Each of these roles—*observer, director, guardian, warrior, lover,* and *leader*—is available to us in any moment. Should we be intent on activating them, we shall *own the moment* in ways we never imagined. Motivation will arise. Life will come back. A vibrancy will emanate through our entire being.

None of us will ever master all these roles in our lives simultaneously. But that does not mean we should neglect them. Today, let us commit to studying these roles and doing our damnedest to enact them with more presence and power.

The sunshine of enlightenment spreads to those who understand that the moments of our lives must not go unnoticed and unlived. We can feel these warm rays of hope if we make the committed choice not to detach from our lives in any way. We mustn't avoid this day's reality or wish for a better one. We must learn to live in reverence to the moment and all we have been given *by* it and all we choose to give *to* it. We can choose our roles and responses to the world so, over time, our character and destiny are forged purposefully. From these efforts, we shall rediscover the immensity and freedom and gift that is each and every divine moment spent alive.

Declaration II

WE SHALL RECLAIM
OUR AGENDA

*The day is always his who works
with serenity and great aims.*

RALPH WALDO EMERSON

HUMAN NATURE STEERS US TOWARD SELF-RELIANCE and freedom. Nothing burns more fiercely in our soul than the desire to be ourselves and pursue our dreams. And so the great joys in life come when we are spontaneous and authentic each day while engaging in activities that we care about. And the great miseries of life come when too many days stack up where we are conforming and posing while doing things we have no passion for.

In these truths, we find a unit for measuring how our freedom is being expressed or not expressed: our individual *days*. Did we spend today being ourselves, expressing our true voice and sincere feelings and innate power? Did we spend the vast majority of the day doing meaningful activities rather than being slave to distraction or useless endeavor?

Life has a way of being easily torn from us day by day. We forget what we want and get distracted. We do what others tell us to do. We say yes to so many things that we end up with no time to do the things that matter to us. This is the reality of the masses.

But freedom and greatness belong to those who master their day. They have an entirely different level of control over the agenda and direction of their life. Their days mean something to them because they know each day gathers force toward a particular destiny. It's as though they imagined themselves standing before their Creator at the end of their lives and having to answer His questions:

Did you use the time I gifted you each day to be a purposeful being?
Did you follow your own path and make your time count?
How faithfully did you tend to the dream I sowed in your soul?

It's as though they awoke each day knowing these questions would come. It's as though each morning they hurled a shining Spear of Purpose far into the fields of the future and then made their mission to go pick it up and throw it once more forward. In their daily struggles to reach the goal, they were focused, unbending, diligent. If they ever felt lost, they had the presence of mind to stop and think, "Am I on the right path? Am I moving forward to what I desire?" If they found themselves sidetracked in the valley of despair and distraction, they knew to lift their head, to climb to a high vantage point, to see where their journey was leading them and if it was where they desired to go, to look for that shining Spear and reorient themselves to it, to find once more the horizon line of their greater destiny. They carried on this way with stunning commitment. They had their own aim in life, and they awoke each day loyal to that cause and ablaze with passion for it. They never let up, despite the struggle and hardship, always thrusting their intent into the distance, always seeking it, always finding a way over or through any obstacle until they ended up either in the land of their dreams or with the angels for having died trying.

What they did not do was waste their days meandering about or marching under the banner of someone else's ambitions.

Contrast their life agenda with the world's stragglers and complainers, who are undirected, passionless, and afraid of work. They fail to cast their intention into the world, or if they do, they allow themselves to be distracted rather than follow their desires to the end. They fail to peer above their immediate tasks to see where they were headed, preferring the illusory sense of progress at having checked off some trifling task. They are too fearful or too lazy or too pulled by the clatter of other people's demands to chase their own dream. They do not strive with real desire and discipline. They make excuse after excuse and tell story after story about why they cannot advance or scale the mountain. They feel no responsibility to fully activate their latent powers. They live unconsciously or in quiet denial, unable to face the truth that their own life agenda is strangely absent or insignificant.

And so the mark of greatness will never be seared into their soul because they did not stay true and faithful to themselves or their mission.

We are one or the other: the striver with the Spear of Purpose or the distracted straggler with the excuse. Which will be our reality? Shall we allow ourselves to be directionless in life, ripped from any purpose by the demands of others and all the distractions of the world? Or shall we finally get serious about the fact that our days will become weeks and weeks will become months and months will become years and decades and a lifetime either won or lost, joyful or regretful, purposeful or squandered?

Let us make this day the day we take back our life's agenda from the grips of conformity and distraction. Let us have our aim in life and move toward it swiftly and diligently. Let us not forget that our simple efforts and daily triumphs can gather weight and motion to become an unstoppable force toward a focused and free life.

We can design our life agendas so that our daily planner is no longer the object of resentment but, rather, a thing of beauty: a stunning log of our enjoyment of life and progress toward freedom and transcendence. We can emancipate our schedules from meaningless tasks and, in the process, lift ourselves to higher standards and higher planes of joy and purpose. We can, through conscious design and vigilant protection of our time and agenda, take back our destiny and make each day artful and fulfilling.

But to do so, we must take a long, unflinching look at our habit of giving our lives and agendas over to others or to meaningless things. We have to say *no* more often. We have to focus more. We have to fight harder to safeguard our time and our dreams and our souls.

Let us now get serious about our days and who we are becoming because of them. Let's get serious about the aim and enjoyment of a meaningful life. It is time to value the hour once more and refuse to give up our lives to the world's distractions and nonsense. It is time to make our own way and get back our day. For this, we declare: *We Shall Reclaim Our Agenda.*

STRIPPED FROM OUR PATH

Few would know or admit if they lacked command of their overall life agenda. How could we tell? What signs would indicate that we are off our unique path in life? There are stark realities and subtle hints.

If there is a lack of true expression, enduring joy, vibrancy, and satisfaction in life, then clearly our agenda has been compromised. For who would plan a life marked with conformity, boredom, fatigue, and dissatisfaction?

If there is a constant shirking of one's dreams out of fear of failure, a suffering sadness in everyday life, or a consistent lack of progress toward one's own clear path, then clearly we are not in charge of our daily emotions and direction.

We can further ask, "Have I become so like others at work that I am not myself? Am I acting like someone else in order to please my parents or friends or lover? Do I believe things and behave in ways that are unexamined, causing me problems, or not a true part of my soul? Do I feel the people around me have no idea who I am or what I want? Did I follow other people without true reflection on what I wanted, and that's why I have this job, or study this topic, or engage in this hobby, or feel trapped in this way of life?"

That is it, the ultimate tell: feeling *trapped*. Should a person feel caged in any aspect of their life, it is an obvious reveal that they have not been owning their life agenda but rather they have been suffering the chains of conformity. They have been catering to everyone else, slave to the prevailing ideas or expectations of others, playing a game they never wanted to be a part of.

The subtler sign is how we consistently *feel* about our lives. If we obtain everything we think we need and every indication says life *should* be satisfying, yet something still feels *"off,"* then we know there is a problem.

If someone asks, *"How are you?"* and we cannot feel a genuinely happy response immediately rise within us, what does that say? It says we are *off* our unique path in life.

This is especially true if, contemplating the question seriously, we find ourselves replying with a mundane lie like, "Oh, well, I guess . . . I'm . . . *fine.*"

Fine is the calling card of conformity.

Things are merely *fine* in life when passion has been slowly bled from our veins. Things are *fine* when we are bored stiff. Things are *fine* when we've done what they told us to do, and we're sick and tired of it. Things are *fine* when we have been marching to the beat of someone else's song for far too long. Things are *fine* when we are aching for more adventure, more passion, more intimacy, more creative expression, more contribution, more drive, more independence, more freedom, more *life in our days*. If we are merely fine, we are not alive. Should we not be *amazing, excited, thrilled, fantastic, phenomenal, beyond grateful?*

Another subtle sign of trouble is that we feel regularly *silent* about things that matter to us. If we want something but we do not ask for it, this means we'll likely accept whatever we are told to do or whatever shows up on life's door.

We must ask: *"Does the world have a sense of who I am? Do my family and friends know who I am and what I truly desire from life? Do my peers and leaders know what I truly want to learn, to work toward, to contribute?"* If we answer with a *no*, then clearly we are not being ourselves or speaking up for ourselves. Such silence reveals fear of rejection or an unhealthy level of need to fit in to what "they" want for us.

> *In this conformist silence there is nothingness—*
> *no sound of life, no pulsing and cracking*
> *and thunder of individuality.*

In such silence, the suffering settles in. Let us never forget that speaking up for ourselves and telling the world what we want and desire is a fundamental practice of a free life.

The final clear indication that someone's life agenda is not their own is constant lack of focus. It is that terrible and never-ending distraction of the modern world that is stealing purpose and progress from our lives. It's becoming a defining hour of humanity, where we either take back our attention or risk becoming emotionally addicted to our technology, to devices that somehow, though they have neither soul or intent, control us more than we control them. Humankind is fast becoming a slave to its own tools. Hours of the day seep away checking in, updating, and swiping, to what end? It's as if we are adrift in a digital stream we never consciously chose to wade into. And we are starting to drown. No sooner do we set out on a *meaningful* task than we feel compelled to look at something irrelevant. We barely make it through a single day without suffering browser blackout or app amnesia—those long gaps in the day when we are lost in a long chain of clicks and swipes that steal our momentum and leave no trace of real purpose or accomplishment.

Yet so many people look effective, so busy with so many tasks, tracking everything unimportant to infinite degrees. In this age of the quantified self, we measure how many hours we slept, steps we took, calories we burned, pages we viewed. We document our every personal move in photos and videos. Yet we know nothing about ourselves. We spend more time checking our stats than our souls. We mine our life experience for data but not depth. We have all these numbers to improve but no idea how to dial back the numbness. As much as we check in, we are checking out of our own lives and becoming voyeuristic, peering gape-mouthed into the sordid details of other people's lives in order to feel connected or entertained.

If we are to measure and monitor and improve anything, let it be our story, our character, and our conduct—a mindfulness of who we are and how we are experiencing and relating with the world. Reclaiming our life agenda is about asking, "Am I proud of who I am and the person I am becoming? Am I happy with what I am doing and contributing to the world? Have I felt grateful for this day and its opportunities, and have I directed myself purposefully so that I can live my highest truth and serve my highest good?" Let us check in on ourselves in these ways, for in the end, these are the only measures that matter.

Our defining moment will come as we either continue to slide into the oblivion of the deep digital stream, clicking and swiping and drowning in distraction, or take a higher vantage point apart from all the noise and, finally, after all this time, choose to refocus on what really matters in life.

Let us boldly ask what it says about ourselves if we cannot pull back from our addiction to digital distractions. For it is an addiction; we are no better off than the alcoholic who cannot avoid the bar or the gambler the casino. Those with a compulsion to constantly check in have lives like this: They awake each day and their first act is to review the messages left by others, always terrified that they may have missed something that someone else wanted on a whim just hours or minutes ago. Their second effort is to divide up their day based not on what they should accomplish in pursuit of their dreams but, rather, on the hours they must spend responding to the needs and requests of others. They reply with equal frenzy and devotion to one and all, to both influencers and idiots, their addiction to meet others' demands making no distinction, giving no priority. All day, they are busy accomplishing nothing but responding to everything. There is no vision, only reaction—a self-imposed terror that they are falling behind. Their aim in life, if we can call it that, is to "get through" it all, to "catch up" in a rat race that they should never have entered and will never win.

This needn't be our fate should we have the courage to take back the responsibility of running our own lives and advancing once more toward meaningful goals every single day no matter what. We must choose this day to finally be more intentional with what we want and what shall deserve our golden attention.

CLARITY ON WHAT IS MEANINGFUL

 What will give us a sense that we are one more in command of our life's agenda? *Clarity. Direction. Progress.*

We begin developing clarity about the current state of our life's agenda by realizing that all human experience is segmented into two fields: meaningful activities and nonmeaningful activities. This forces a clear distinction when evaluating our days. *Do I find what I am doing each day of my life meaningful? Is all this busywork in line with what I feel is my life's work?* These are the questions of the self-determined. Such questions make us reevaluate everything—every task, responsibility, and opportunity that is laid before us by the world must now be questioned as to whether or not it aligns with our goals, whether or not it enlivens us, whether or not it allows us to feel fulfilled. To those activities that come up short, we must be unblinking and once and for all release our belief that we must be doing them.

Some will moan at this work. They will say, "But I do not like my answers. You do not understand. I have to do this terrible job. My workday is not my choice." To those who believe this, only time and maturity will help them uncover the truth: work, just like our emotions, is ultimately a choice. Whether or not we wield that power is up to us. If we don't like the work we are doing, we have three choices:

Continue hating what we do;

Change our perspective and find meaning and joy in our current tasks; or

Quit the dispassionate work and seek out what will make our soul sing.

One would hope everyone would, at some point, and as soon as responsibly possible, choose the last option.

Do we have to quit every job we hate? No. Surely, we could stay in any job and succeed—greatness can be cultivated in the soil of any experience. But we all know that the seeds of greatness grow faster in the hearts of those doing work they love than in the bitter hearts of those enslaved by work they despise.

Some give their entire lives away to work they dislike because they never have the resolve to ask, "What if I were free and strong enough to go find something more engaging and fulfilling? What if the world isn't giving me what I want because, based on all my distractions and lack of discipline toward a goal, it's simply unclear what I am asking for?" In such bold questions we unsettle ourselves and unleash a new kind of desire and strength within.

SETTING A DIRECTION:
A Written Manifesto

We must go further. Beyond evaluating our current life experience and becoming clear as to whether or not our days' efforts are meaningful to us, we must set a new and more proactive course for our lives.

What will our mission be from this moment forward?

What will be our plan of action?

What steps must be taken?

These questions are not a philosophical suggestion. We should sit down now with pen in hand and write out the focus and direction of our lives from now forward. Lacking our own declarations and directives in life—written down, reviewed, updated, lived from—we can only fall into the herd. We end up where "they" take us, where they want us, wherever the wind blows us, regardless of our hopes and intent. Such a life is not one we want.

So now, in these magical moments of our lives bursting with fire and choice, let us sit and write. Let us take back our day tomorrow by scribing our dreams tonight. Let us ask:

What am I *really* after in life?

What do I *truly* want to create and contribute?

What kind of person do I want to show the world each day?

What types of persons shall I love and enjoy life with?

What great cause will keep me going when I feel weak or distracted?

What shall be my ultimate legacy?

What steps must I take to begin and sustain these efforts?

What will I orient my days to accomplishing this week? This month? This year?

Yes, we must write these things down in what will be our own manifesto, our own written declaration of what our lives are to be about.

Those who lack such a written document must stop fooling themselves and thinking *they* are in charge of their lives. For without such self-direction, we are but sad vessels captained by conformity. Intentions and occasional musings about life are insufficient for keeping anyone from conforming or losing their days to distraction. There is a reason nations write out and follow their declarations, constitutions, and laws. No matter how strong a society, no matter its intent or culture or popular will, without written directives all is lost in the randomness of human behavior. That is why we must write and that is why we must revisit our manifestos and that is why we must act in alignment to the agenda we have set for ourselves.

After all this writing is done, let us rise tomorrow and forge the day and week to begin moving toward and accomplishing these things. Let us fight for these things. Let us use the morning to remind ourselves what we are after and to write any specific goals for the day, dedicating time in that first golden hour to planning out our schedule. That precious first hour must not be squandered, for our evening's dreams can easily be forgotten in daylight. We must use the virgin morning to shape a schedule that is ours before the world shoves its corrupt needs in our direction. Yes, rise in the morning and write some more. *Who will I be today? What dreams will I chase? What will I create and accomplish no matter what? Who will I give value, love, or appreciation to? What will I do or experience that will help me feel fulfilled and grateful when I rest my head to pillow later tonight?*

This is called living intentionally and independently. This is how motivated persons live. This is manifesting a freer life. Everything else is wishing and hoping, a steady decline into mediocrity, the dead boring drumbeat of the reactive and unconscious life.

PROGRESS DESPITE OBLIGATION

For some, this talk of taking back our lives will seem out of reach, not because they question their potential but rather because they feel obligated to subjugate it for others. They say, "You do not understand; I have to meet the needs of everyone else. My day is not my choice because everyone around me must be loved and cared for. I must sacrifice my dreams and pursuit of meaningful things at the altar of love or obligation. I have to please everyone else so I cannot progress or have my own joys and freedom." Time, maturity, and that great revelation that is choice are also needed for such persons.

No one around us can tear us from progressing toward our dreams.
Believing otherwise is accepting the role of victim in life.
Our day is ultimately our choice.

And so what can be done? Must we leave everyone who needs us so that we can have the lives we desire? Perhaps the more mature choice is to learn new ways to protect our desires and dreams while fulfilling our chosen roles in life. We can be good mothers and still strive diligently each day toward our dreams. We can be good leaders who help others achieve more while still striving diligently toward our day's goals.

In dealing with the needs of others while maintaining our life's agenda, we must learn the stunning power of *no*. There is no rule written anywhere that says we must say *yes* to every passing request that crosses our desks or burns in our ears from a crying whiner.

This is not to say we cannot be loving and responsible to those who need us and when it brings us joy. If loving and caring for specific people is exactly what we find meaningful, then we must do just that. Taking the girls to soccer is not a distraction if it brings meaning to our days. However, we must not allow the world's distractions, casual loiterers, or random opportunities to constantly rob us of our intended day.

For most, not knowing how to say *no* is where their lives decline into a thicket of stress and unhappiness. These individuals are easy to spot, as they constantly take on the role of victim to the world's desires. Their life appears to be an industrial slog, ticking off the tasks handed to them by others. They may appear frazzled and frenetic, choked in the tightening clutch of deadlines they did not choose or plan. They often appear to be awaiting instruction and direction, thus their schedule is really more holding pattern than action plan. They get stuck in life because they never rise above their timid desires to please others. Their only true effort is to fit into the wants and schedules of the world and so there is no purposeful art or arc to their week, year, decade, or life. Theirs is a groaning, grueling life under the weight of other people's control and expectations.

We all face the eternal drama of balancing our personal needs and ambitions with those of the people we love, lead, and serve. But we mustn't succumb to victimhood. Other people will always demand our time and attention, including people we love and care about. Our parents will want our ear more often than we want to give it. Our friends and neighbors will call on us for parties and meetings. We will have obligations from our church, political party, and volunteer organizations. We'll have bosses who expect around-the-clock access and instant response.

But how shall we respond to such requests? If we say *yes* to all of them, we will be buried. Our only choice is to say *no*, and to say it *often*, to say it *more* than we like or anyone else likes. The only exceptions should be in the cases in which we find saying *yes* to be personally and socially meaningful and part of our advance toward our ideal lives.

Vigilance will be needed because there will always be those needy few who can smell our desire to please. They will attack like black ravens from the sky, diving again and again as they devour our lives piece by piece. This is the guy at the office who is constantly asking for another random favor, the former girlfriend always calling with drama and in need of rescue, the entitled employee whom we helped once and now refuses to lift a finger to do real work. These people will keep coming at us and they do not care about our agenda or destiny. Their opportunism will plague us should we not be intentional in saying *no* and *no* and *no*. We must learn to reply artfully and often forcefully to those who are always saying, "I'm so sorry to have to ask you for one more little favor." To them, let us reply, "I cannot help right now. I have plans that cannot wait or accommodate your sudden emergency."

In saying this, we need not apologize any more than we need to apologize to the person who runs into our car when we had the right of way. We can be artful if we must: "I do wish I could help, but unfortunately I am unable to get to your last-minute request because my plate is full with long-ago scheduled activities and projects that that I have already committed to."

How we handle the enemies of our own progress speaks to our character and independence. We are doomed if we subordinate our day's agenda to their every request or crisis. In meeting their needs, which are usually false deadlines or urgencies created only by their lack of preparation or responsibility, we lose an irrecoverable hour that could have propelled our own life forward. For these reasons, we must reclaim our agenda with a forceful grip. We must look to the world's random pushy people, the countless needy people, the people not on our list of those we want to love, care for, and attend to. It cannot be overstated: *We must not fear saying, "No, I cannot help you now."*

And so let us decide that we will not let other people's fire drills result in daily drills of us scratching off our dreams. The demands of the whimsically needy or the terminally ill-prepared are not our issue. Their lives are not our responsibility.

Owning this life truth is freeing: *I am not in charge or responsible for the wrecks others have created in their lives and I do not need to save everyone in my life.*

What can we expect for standing tough and true at the gates of our agenda? What happens when we say *no?* Most will understand, and over time most will come to respect us and leave us alone.

But let us not delude ourselves: There will be a small contingent of people who will become angry. They won't like our free will and independence. They will try to ridicule or guilt us. They may ask, *"Who the hell do you think you are?"* They may feel scorned and launch bitter campaigns to make us their pawns once more, to force or gently steer us back into their grasp, to deliver us back into their concept of how we should treat them. Many will argue that we *owe* them a permanent debt for their love and sacrifice. "How dare you refuse me? How can you leave me on my own? After I've done so much for you, how can you not grant me this one small thing?" In the face of such wheedling, we mustn't compromise else we risk being pulled into an ever-growing sticky web of demands. We shall discover that the more often we say *no,* the more likely people will find someone else to pester or they will become more self-reliant in the vacuum of our constant availability.

Yes, we will arouse antagonism, lose favor, break loyalties, and imperil our popularity. It will happen more and more as we gain greater and greater will and freedom in life. So be it.

No great person ever made history without having guilt thrown at them or suffering some backlash from those who didn't like or appreciate their independence, discipline, or single-mindedness.

So let the petty ones complain. Let them tremble with silly anxiety or anger. After days and weeks and months of protecting our turf, refusing to give in to guilt or pressure, stating convincingly that we have our own dreams to chase, we will find that the demanding bullies and unaware idiots finally have left us alone. Then, liberated from the social oppression that is others' distracting demands, we are free, liberated to create and design our own lives in the newly opened white space of time. *The more we say no to demanding people, the more life opens up to pursue our passions and happiness and to serve and spend time with those we love.*

But what shall be done when it is our loved ones who constantly need us or tear us from our path? Let us be patient with them, but let us be real. We must artfully deal with anyone who derails the day's mission, including family. For the most part, this simply means asking for our space during blocks of time during the day. It is saying to our young boy, "Son, your mother needs the next two hours to focus on a very important project that means a lot to her. Please do not go into her office." Once this is said, it is only mature parenting that will prevent the boy from entering the room—we must stand our ground. We can train our children or our teammates that when our office door is closed, they should not enter unless in emergency. We can lovingly request that our spouse give us an hour each evening to read or meditate or create art. We can say *no* to the parties, the gatherings, the formal functions that we feel so obligated to attend. There may be scowls and long faces at first, but over time people will realize we are *persons of purpose* and they will give us room, knowing that the more they respect our schedule, the more likely we will find and make the time to be with them.

Our goal is not to become cold or unavailable. No, it is to protect our sanity, progress, and freedom. It is worth repeating that we can and should give time and attention to those we love and lead—*when we desire to do so*. Being good to those around us is right and responsible, but never at the cost of our own long-term sanity or dreams. Besides, is it not true that by saying *no* more to what is wrong, we are left with more time to give loving attention to those close to us?

Some ask, "Should we not compromise? Can there be no middle ground between our desires and the needs of those around us?" Perhaps. But there is a difference between adding a few tasks onto the day's schedule to serve others and *compromising our entire life agenda*. When it comes to forgoing our true passions and path in life to please others, we must never compromise. Compromise means giving something away, something in exchange for another's willingness to do the same. But we shall not give an entire piece of our dream nor a decade of our lives over to anyone. Yes, we can help and love others on our way to Personal Freedom. But we mustn't give away so much time that our freedom itself is fully compromised. We can meet our real responsibilities and care for our loved ones, but our own progress must never falter or stop, lest we become slave to the world. If in aiding others, we kill our own dreams, then it is merely our ego seeking to make a false martyr of ourselves.

We must keep the big picture in mind. A million dreams have died because compromising souls repeated the lie of the weak: "I'm okay with putting off my needs and dream another few years, because people need me." Shall we do nothing but reply to the needs of others all day until, in the day's final hours, we retreat to our beds, exhausted by the madness, not one step closer to what we wanted in life, so that we can sleep restlessly only to awake once more in a world determined by others rather than by ourselves? No, let us not compromise our dreams or barter our destiny hour by hour.

If we can see a dream in the distance,
let us move toward it with real force, will, and consistency.

To do less is to let the dream weaken and die. We can support our loved ones for a while, stepping in, helping out—but that does not require us to bring our dreams to a full *stop*. Every day we can do *something* to advance our own agenda.

Perhaps it is also time to stop seeing others as obstacles to our dreams but rather as collaborators. Have we sat down our loved ones and told them what we truly desire of life and why? Have we asked our teams to help brainstorm new ways to work together so that all our desires can be met? Are we engaging others enough so that they will be supportive and participative in our life's pursuits? Real progress often comes in our lives once we make people our allies in accomplishment.

THE GREAT RECLAMATION

Each day we have a choice to go with the wants and whims of the world or to chart our own course. If we abandon self-determination, we are left adrift in a chaotic sea and the only things on the horizon are swells of boredom or suffering. And so our attitude each morning must be that *this* is our day, no matter what. If we can start with that intention, if we develop clarity and write our own manifestos and plans and we execute them with heart and discipline, if we stick to it and fight it through and stay in charge, we suddenly find ourselves one day back at the helm, happy, motivated, *alive*.

Declaration III

WE SHALL DEFEAT
OUR DEMONS

*A person who doubts himself is like a man who would enlist
in the ranks of his enemies and bear arms against himself.*

ALEXANDRE DUMAS

As we gain greater presence and purpose in life,
we become more attuned to our vitality and strength.
We also become more aware of the profound ways in which
we limit ourselves. We come to realize that our thoughts,
more so than our circumstances, sabotage our freedom and
success. We are the ones who allow our insecurities and
fears to grow into the tidal waves of worry that wash our
dreams away. We are the ones who constantly delay our
own progress, quitting just as the hour demands courageous action. We are the ones separating ourselves from
others so that we needn't risk real connection or so that we
can feel better than them.

None of us wants to look in the mirror and realize that
the person looking back is the cause of such frustration.

We would rather smile at the reflection and be proud of its courage. We want to see ourselves as free and motivated masters of our own lives. Yet a quick glance into our own tired eyes often reveals a knowledge that we are standing in our own way. Too often we find ourselves muttering at the mirror, "You again? Why can't you get your act together and go for what you truly desire? Why aren't you taking more risks, speaking up more, being more consistent, connecting better with people?" These are difficult days when we realize our internal demons are beating us. Those days must come to an end. Now.

Greatness belongs to those who have mastered their internal world. We are all plagued by doubt, but the great nevertheless find faith and begin. We all feel like delaying action, but the great march on. We all want to avoid vulnerability or act superior over others from time to time, but the great consistently demonstrate openness, humility, and love. These few are not lucky; they are simply more intentional and more practiced at defeating their internal demons. That is why they have so much vitality, motivation, and confidence—enlightenment comes to those who free themselves from self-oppression.

Let us choose to make that our aim, and once and for all root out that which holds us back in life. We deserve to be free from all those stirrings within us that compromise our magnificence. For this, let us declare: *We Shall Defeat Our Demons.*

THE ENEMY WITHIN

It is impossible to fight an unknown enemy, so let us first give our challenger a name. As it stands in the way of our own will to advance in life, we shall name it *Defiance*.

To dramatize its effect and our battle against it, we will also give it a shape, a form that we can visualize and seek to destroy. Imagine Defiance as an ugly three-headed serpent that stirs deep in our gut whenever we want to take a risk. When this brute squirms we feel anxiety in our stomach, that awful sense that we are not enough or things might turn out terribly. Its movements make us worry ourselves sick. It makes us feel so weak and distrustful that we stop taking action or connecting with others. It is the organism within that acts from our lowest impulses for self-protection.

No one escapes life without fighting this beast. The woman who never starts her own business because of constant terror is in its grasp. The poor fellow who starts and stops action all his life, never gaining real momentum toward his goals, is being wrecked by it. The egotistical businessperson who sees his teammates as idiots or competitors is being seduced by it.

Any time we set a higher ambition for ourselves, this nasty beast gnaws at us from within, tearing at our confidence and consuming us from the inside out, leaving us fearful and gutless.

Where did Defiance come from and how did it gain its power?

It grew from the seeds of fear fed to us by the tyrants of the world: the cautioners who taught us to favor doubt over faith, the apathetic followers who showed us how to favor delay over action, the cruel who fooled us into choosing artificiality and social withdrawal over authenticity and the desire to approach. In the end, they were one and the same—fear mongers all, tyrants who sowed the seeds of dread deep within us at an early stage. The negative thoughts they planted in our heads fed the beast within, and now it grows in power whenever we hear ourselves think, "I'm not good enough. I better stop doing what I love because I'm scared. I'm not worthy of trust and respect and neither are others." The bullies of the world may have given us these thoughts. But it was our own failure to discontinue them that birthed the internal struggle we face today. With our own weakness and inattention, we have given Defiance its power.

As we become more aware, we learn to sense this beast as separate from our own nature. We can detect when it stirs within us, noticing a sudden wave of tension and stress in our body. We can hear its whines and roars rise from our gut into fear-sharpened thoughts: "I am not *sure!*" "The *timing* may not be right!" "*They* won't understand me or let me win!" We can realize that these feelings in our body and these sounds in our head are not of our highest character but those of an internal voice of Defiance, whom we need not feed anymore.

Defiance can roar all it wants, but we can choose
to ignore it as we might a pesky yapping dog.

It can shift and cause pangs of worry or hatred, but we can calm ourselves by taking control of our own thoughts and actions. With practice, we can exercise total command,

and silence this internal demon once and for all. Should we succeed, we shall begin to reach our full personal power.

TRANSFORM DOUBT WITH FAITH

Defiance is a fierce foe. In order to confront it, let us get to know this foul serpent by understanding the defining character of each of its nasty heads.

Let us imagine the first head of Defiance to resemble that of a pale, sickly eel. We sense it as an *unsure feeling* in the pit of our stomach that rises until we hear an indecisive chain of thoughts in our head. Its sound in our mind is a high, familiar whine, like the voice of an old, tolerated friend who has our ear and uses it only to share her worries and insecurities. Although it may look and sound pathetic, we should not underestimate it. Its sole insidious function is to make us worry ourselves sick so that we might avoid the very risk or effort that would destroy it. For these reasons, we shall name it *Doubt*.

Doubt wakes up when we strive for anything new or better. It recognizes that in those moments when our ambition rises, its very existence is in peril—for should we rise to accomplish our goals with confidence again and again, then it might be destroyed. The only thing Doubt can do to survive is avert our strength by whining and singing its pessimistic song: *I'm not so sure, I'm not so sure, I'm not so sure . . .*

Inevitably, its plaintive tones unsteady most people. They can't handle the incessant worries of Doubt and soon they are trapped in recurring negative thoughts. *I'm not so sure it is time to quit my job. Maybe it's not the right time to move somewhere I would love. She'll probably say no if I ask her on a date. I don't think it's a good idea to follow my passions or to strike out on my own.*

The precise moments when Doubt begins to prevail in our lives are predictable. They happen when our doubting thoughts turn to real words—the moment we begin asking, *"What if . . ."* and then follow the phrase with a negative statement:

What if . . . it doesn't work out?

What if . . . I can't handle it?

What if . . . I'm not good enough?

What if . . . they don't like me?

What if . . . I lose?

What if . . . I can't turn back?

What if . . . they take advantage of me?

These are the questions of a mind poisoned by Doubt, not of our highest self.

It is the *allowance* and *repetition* of doubtful questions that stall most people from living free and fulfilling lives.

There can be no real progress if we incessantly question our own course and capabilities. Yet the greatest damage from Doubt isn't just what we fail to *do;* it is who we fail to *become.* We develop character only through effort, struggle, and learning, none of which we ever choose to endure when Doubt has our ear. Doubt produces only small men and small women, scared of their own shadows—a world of timid worriers who never leap or serve.

So what are we to do?

How does one slay Doubt?

The great sages have taught us that when Doubt has a hold on us, only Faith can tear us from its grasp.

Faith is a deep conviction, a global trust and confidence in our beliefs about what is true. The conviction comes from choice—we choose to believe something and *hold on to that belief tightly*, even in the face of so many unknowns. We have Faith when we can endure sadness or suffering or loss and keep our wits about us, knowing that eventually these things shall pass and good things will return. We have Faith when we believe in our capabilities to succeed.

This belief needn't be overestimations of our current skill or strength. Instead, the most powerful Faith in the world is the humble variety that says, "I believe in my ability to *learn* and figure things out. With enough focus, time, effort, and dedication, I believe I can learn to do what must be done and become who I must become to achieve my dreams." If we carry on with this kind of Faith to learn and live into our potential, then Doubt lies sweating on its deathbed.

So tonight, in the stillness and magic of the last hours, let us grab our journals and write all the reasons we have to believe in ourselves and this world once more. What have we already done in life that we didn't know we could? What reasons can we find to believe that tomorrow we will be better and the world will open up to us? Why will we continue to believe in ourselves and our dreams even amid difficult days? Yes, let us write these things. Let us force ourselves to do this seemingly simple activity now. For in writing our beliefs, Faith itself is strengthened. Then, the next time Doubt rears its ugly head, remember what was written. Remember what we believe. Replace its negative whining with more positive and empowering thoughts. This is the way of those who have mastered their mind.

As we choose Faith again and again throughout our lives, we develop a mental toughness for beating away Doubt. It's as if with each firing of conviction we forge an increasingly powerful, steeled weapon capable of piercing all negative thought. When we practice such power, it becomes something we can firmly grasp and wield in times of need and anxiety. Soon, Faith is our favored weapon and we become invincible against the darkness. We become the warriors of light who have an unshakable sense of self and serenity, who rarely question themselves or Fate, who draw luck and abundance in all they do because they believe the universe favors those with a committed heart and all things are unfolding exactly as it should.

TRANSFORM DELAY WITH ACTION

There is so much at stake for Faith to win in our lives. For if we don't tame the crippling thoughts hatched by Doubt, we awaken an ever greater evil. The second serpent head of Defiance, whose aim is to stop our advance by poisoning us with apathetic and resigned thought, is named after its sole miserable mission: *Delay*.

We can imagine Delay's physical shape as that of a burnt-orange eel with a severe face and a thunderous voice that can shake us from head to toe.

If its brother Doubt breeds uncertainty with its whiny song of concern, Delay engenders real terror. When it strikes us, it feels as if something is ramming its head into our chest. Delay thumps us and screams at us, its calls resonating throughout our very cells. *Wait!* it booms. *Stop!* it shouts. *Don't! Please! Stop! You'll be hurt! You are not ready! Listen to my brother Doubt—the path is unsure! Do no more! Take no action. You will be hurt, I say! Saddened! Embarrassed! Destroyed! Sit! Wait it out or you are doomed! This is not the time!* Delay's voice gets louder as we get closer to action.

Delay makes no effort to woo or seduce us; it is a dictator of terms—*stop or be hurt; wait or risk ruin.* Presented with such dire choices, our mind rarely argues. With internal fears that we may be hurt, rejected, or ruined, why wouldn't we stop? Suddenly moving forward sounds like suicide, and so our minds start crafting masterful arguments for justifying *inaction.* We become severely confident in our negativity in order to protect ourselves, saying things to ourselves and others like, "Well, the conditions aren't perfect yet for me to begin. You can't just rush into things, you know."

And so if life is not progressing fast enough for us, Delay is there. If we have been waiting and waiting for the right time to strike out on our own, to approach a potential lover, to seek a higher position, to start a new project, to actually fight for what we truly want, Delay is there. It is Delay that turns people of action into people of apathy and insignificance. Nothing has done more than Delay to make potentially great men and women miss their moment.

Knowing that we haven't spoken up when we should have,
worked when we should have, fought when we should have,
loved when we should have, lived when we should have—
this is the misery of mankind's inaction,
of Delay celebrating a win over our soul.

So it can be said that Delay is the worse of the two evils—it has destroyed more dreams than Doubt ever could. For even with Doubt awakened and worrying our soul, we can at least act with valor and swiftness when at our best. But we cannot and will not act if Delay is running our conscience.

But there is hope. There always is. Like Doubt has its antidote, so too does Delay. The poisons of fear, apathy, and indolence spread by Delay can be wiped out with the antidote of decisive Action. When we take the initiative despite the trumped-up desires to wait it out in fear, when we pick up the phone to make that important call, walk over to the table to talk to that cute stranger, enroll in that new course, take that risk—these things set off an internal tidal wave of power that subjugates our meeker impulses. Taking decisive action is freeing ourselves from Delay.

Destiny turns its favor toward those who act,
awarding them with success and a heroic recognition in life.

Is it not true that we would have no heroes if, in the moment they were called to action, they decided to wait? All greatness teeters on whether a hero overcomes the terror within and *advances regardless.* The Olympian who trips during the race but gets up and catches up, the bystander who is afraid of the rushing waters but jumps in to save the drowning girl, the whistleblower who knows he'll be fired for calling out a wrong but speaks up anyway. *Heroism is taking action to do important things even when we are afraid.* Cowardice is acting in accordance to our fears when our heart wishes to see us behave more nobly and courageously.

The hope of humanity rests on whether or not Action overrides fear and apathy. So let all this waiting for everything to be perfect, all this creating excuses for why we must delay our own dreams, all this nonsense about why we don't deserve it right now fall to the wayside. Let Action plow through our hesitancies.

We must do the things that we have put off and most fear doing, and we must do them now. Let us sit this very night and compose a list of things we have been delaying in our lives. *What have we yet to begin?* Where did we stall our next move because of Delay and what must be done to pick up the torch of progress once more? Being keen to these types of questions makes us stronger men and women. Having a plan and acting on it to advance our lives, regardless of the terror within, makes us legend.

TRANSFORM DIVISION WITH LOVE

If worry and waiting were not misery enough, the third serpent head of Defiance acts to ensure we suffer *alone*. This one poisons us with the venom of separation, making our blood and our behavior run cold. It makes us distant, intolerant, or hateful toward others. It inflates our ego to feel different than others, more special, stronger, or weaker than they. This demon is more self-assured and sinister than its brethren. Let us imagine it as an eyeless, jet-black serpent head. Its goal is to shred our humanity by making us go blind to the good in others. We'll name it *Division*.

Division attacks our hearts and is the reason for a sickened society. Whenever we refuse to feel vulnerable or loving toward another, this is Division at work. And whenever we feel that everyone around us is an idiot, insufficient, or unworthy of trust or respect, this is Division once more. All of our social angst and intolerances stem from Division— that loneliness, disconnection, fear, or anger toward others is a result of its poisons corrupting our mind and humanity.

As Division is devoid of empathy or sympathy for others, its ultimate victory is the moment when we no longer see one another's humanity—when we objectify, dismiss, or disregard another individual's value and rights. Its ugliest form is to blame for the wars, the rapes, the brutality, the darkest stains on humankind's history.

In everyday life, this demon is most noticeable when it sparks our impatience, contempt, and withdrawal. Its toxins make us feel high-minded and pretentious, as if we should live above, and insulated from, others; as if we were somehow more special than our brothers, sisters, friends, and associates. Criticism, nitpicking, disparagement, and wrath become our tools for relating to those stronger or weaker than we perceive ourselves.

We can also sense it easily when we become judgmental or cannot safely feel love for another nor sense oneness with them. This is the mother with an extraordinary daughter who sees only her flaws, the impatient boss who thinks everyone is stupid and slow, the man who never loves because he thinks he's too weird or different from the norm.

> *Division's poison, then, is antisocial venom*
> *that courses through us and clouds the innate*
> *emotional, social, and spiritual intelligence*
> *that would otherwise lead us universally*
> *to connection with others and to Love.*

Division, then, is the great destroyer of our relationships, the breeder of all social ills, and the cause for our indifference and aloofness toward others.

Even if we should find the inner strength and resolve to banish Doubt and Delay from our lives, our destiny will still fail if we let Division have its way. Without social care and connection, even Faith and Action can become corrupt or inadequate. This is the confident, successful man who ends up alone and regretful, triumphant in achievement but trailing the wreckage of failed marriages and friendships. We see it in the tale of the woman who, instead of finding sisterhood, finds jealousy and bitterness among her peers. It's the child who shuts down, becomes violent, and ends up in prison because he couldn't find connection and compassion for others.

What can be done?

> *We must inject into our lives the strongest antivenom*
> *known to humankind, the cure of all evils and pains,*
> *the divine course that speeds all recovery and fuels*
> *all of humanity's hope and strength and joy: LOVE.*

Love is the antidote to Division. Its warm intent flows through our veins and floods the chasms between us, sweeping away the detritus of judgment, anger, and hatred. The more we open the floodgates, the more power we have. In our opening to love, all the chemicals of evil and discord are washed away, and the inner serpent of solitude along with them.

Who have we been avoiding or mistreating because of Division?

What parts of ourselves have we shut down out of fear that we would be deemed too different, unworthy, or unlovable?

We must be aware enough to answer such questions and mature enough to seek resolution. Fortunately, Love is in our nature and the most abundant resource in the universe, for it created and lives in all things. All we must do now is allow it back into our lives and direct it toward others.

Unlike Faith and Action—ingredients willed to life by our choice—Love lives both *within* and *beyond* us. Love is everywhere, the Divine's cosmic thread, woven through all that we see and sense. As we learn to follow and pull from this common thread, we recognize the oneness of which we are all part. We see that we are all made of the same purity, fighting the same demons, marching in our own ways to our own freedoms, all journeying back to Love.

Love completes our healing. For we can have all the Faith and Action in the world, but without Love there is no strength. It is Love that gives Faith its raw and divine powers, Love that causes us to be courageous, to take actions that we would never take for ourselves.

When Love springs unfiltered from our hearts, then the last impulse of Defiance is vanquished.

Love is always the final and most complete cure to our inner demons.

THE SWORD OF COURAGE

We now know Defiance and its three serpent heads:

Doubt questions our worth and course of action.

Delay breeds indolence.

Division closes the mind and heart.

In one creature, we find the cause of most human misery; *for it is the lack of certainty, activity, and humanity that derails our destiny.*

It would be naïve to believe that we can ever vanquish Defiance once and for all. Even if we defeat it in the moments that matter most in our lives—*and this we must do*—it will still return. Defiance is a noxious weed planted in us by a society in constant dis-ease, often germinating from our own insecurity and neglect. It grows fast and keeps returning, sending out its brambles and runners throughout our lives. The only sure method of eradication is our constant persistence in pulling it out by its roots. This is an effort we must commit to, and then recommit to daily. Happily, we know we are able to beat Defiance back with Faith, Action, and Love.

Just as we have given Defiance form, we can do the same for our weapon against it. Let us imagine our one needed weapon against our internal terrors as the Sword of Courage. It is a sword of unbending steel forged from that remarkable triumvirate—a strong hilt formed of Faith, and an indestructible blade of Action on one edge and Love on the other. Let us remember this image of Courage the next time Defiance resists our progress, and use it to overpower the enemy. The moments when we are able to wield Courage are the moments that become the most defining in our lives.

All great people of history, all the heroes and leaders and innovators who lit humanity's way out of darkness and ignorance, forged within themselves the courage to overcome their internal conflicts when it mattered most. In many ways, they are just like us: They worried. They procrastinated. They sometimes had lower opinions of their fellow human beings. But what made them celebrated, what pushed society forward, what gave birth to their legend, was their sheer will to overcome such impulses and to *faithfully*, *actively*, and *lovingly* fight for a better life for themselves and others. Let us learn from them, let us master ourselves, and let us now add our own chapter of courage to the good book of humanity.

DECLARATION IV

WE SHALL ADVANCE
WITH ABANDON

Cowards die many times before their deaths;
The valiant never taste of death but once.

WILLIAM SHAKESPEARE,
Julius Caesar

A S WE OVERCOME FEAR AND DEFEAT OUR INTERNAL demons, we must recalibrate our entire mindset toward advancement. Ours must become a life of courageous action and perpetual progress.

The majority of the world's people are not advancing at the speed of which they are capable. They have not sought self-mastery and so they lack the personal power to direct their energies. Wrong thinking and weak wills are preventing them from extending themselves fully toward their dreams. It is like watching a cheetah stroll lazily all its life, never powerfully stretching and leaping at the staggering speed within its potential.

To reclaim our power, we must seek an immediate shift in our belief about how influential we can be in shaping our reality. We must understand that nothing in life, including our circumstances or potential, is fixed. Instead, we must believe that we can bend reality to our own preferences, crafting the lives we desire through disciplined learning and initiative. We mustn't wait for permission or perfect timing any longer. Instead we must be courageous and self-reliant, moving forward at a moment's notice. We must see struggle as positive and necessary for our growth and ability to innovate and serve. And we must know all that we need is accessible in the Now—there is abundance in this world to be had, and everything we need to begin the great quest toward a free and fulfilling life is already within us. Should we live from these beliefs, then we shall reach levels of motivation and happiness undreamed of by the timid masses.

Our challenge is that we have been conditioned to believe the opposite of these things—that bold action or swift progress is somehow dangerous or reckless. But a certain degree of insanity and recklessness is *necessary* to advance or innovate anything, to make any new or remarkable or meaningful contributions. What great thing was ever accomplished without a little recklessness? So-called recklessness was required for the extraordinary to happen: crossing the oceans, ending slavery, rocketing man into space, building skyscrapers, decoding the genome, starting new businesses, and innovating entire industries. It *is* reckless to try something that has never been done, to move against convention, to begin before all conditions are good and preparations are perfected. But the bold know that to win, one must first *begin*. They also deeply understand that a degree of risk is inevitable and necessary should there be any real reward. Yes, any plunge into the unknown is reckless—but that's where the treasure lies.

Sadly, even intelligent conversations about success today are shrouded in limiting advice. How many people have lost all grand ambitions for change and greatness by heeding the advice of the "realists" and the standard-bearers of the status quo, who tell us to set safe and "smart" goals? But smart goals almost always end up being small goals, utterly predictable and absurdly measured small plans for small people who need certainty and safety to such a degree they cannot wade into the wide territory of the unknown where real vision and progress lives. No great innovation or human leap forward came from a predictable path or an idea that was immediately "attainable" or "realistic." It's rare that these types of goals ever spark the imagination or fire the will of the human spirit.

We live in a culture flooded with tasks and spreadsheets and work plans that inspire no heart, no drive, no courage. Should we want true change and a life of our own, we must not, under any circumstances, allow ourselves to settle on a vision or a calling or a change in any arena that is contrived by popular opinion versus our own heart. A truly free person does not fear bringing forth a desire that is unbounded and even scares them a little bit, something that will demand the best of themselves, that might rattle them but take them out of their own orbit and into the stratosphere of the remarkable.

Our destiny hinges on a mindset for bold action. We gain power from again and again allowing ourselves to choose the kind of recklessness that allows us to be vulnerable, genuine, and brave in pursuit of our dreams. When our hearts yearn for action and growth, we should care little about what society says is possible or prudent. Let us judge for ourselves what is worth the risk. Let us decide what progress really means in life, as it surely means more than inching along like snails. Let us decide to take our first steps without knowing how the journey will turn out. If that defines us as reckless and crazy, then let us accept that fate and celebrate the fact that we shall not be cowards. Let us declare: *We Shall Advance with Abandon*.

REALITY IS BENDABLE

This power begins with developing a *mindset* for real momentum.

The first mark of such a mindset is believing that *reality is bendable to our will*. Those who lack this belief never advance with great power and constancy.

Free and courageous people do not avoid their current circumstances but see them as temporary. To those who are self-reliant, reality is not fixed but rather fickle and moldable. They see their entire existence as something that can be shaped, toyed with, vastly improved. Nothing that exists today must exist forever. New ideas and new worlds can replace all that is known. Their only commitment is to creating the future they have imagined for themselves and their loved ones.

The great say, "Reality can be shaped and changed by my direct actions, and so I will act with constancy to forge my ideal life." To them, their *vision* trumps reality; their dreams have more weight than their circumstances because they know circumstances are alterable with enough sweat and toil and dedication.

Victims and quitters take a different view. They often think their reality is fixed, determined by others outside themselves, immutable. For them, reality is all there is. They tell themselves, "Tomorrow is fated to be exactly like today and the days that came before it. There is nothing I can do; this is my reality. This is just the way it is, and always will be. Today is merely something to plod through." What matters to them is surviving life, not shaping it.

Consumed by the belief that nothing changes, these people have no cause to act or advance. Nor do they have big visions for themselves. What would be the point? They think, "Well, if I can't change anything, I'll just settle for what random circumstance gives to me."

Those with this mindset seem to have missed the large sign we should have all crossed on our road to maturity:

YOU ARE RESPONSIBLE FOR YOUR REALITY.

DECIDE WHAT YOU WANT OF THE WORLD
AND GO MAKE IT HAPPEN.

NO CLARITY, NO CHANGE; NO GOALS, NO GROWTH.

Ultimately, those sad souls who believe that reality cannot be shaped do very little in life and will unfortunately be judged as weak, irresponsible, or forgettable.

If nature and humankind's ascent has proven anything, it is that real change is possible and inevitable, and should we direct it to improve our life and our species, it is our salvation.

Let us take this truth into our minds and ask, "What of my reality do I like and dislike? What areas of my life have I been taking a backseat on, hoping they would get better but failing to change my own reality? What would have to change—no, what would *I* have to change—in order to feel more engaged, enthusiastic, and fulfilled with my life?" These simple questions have the power to reconnect us with our lives and ultimately with our power.

ACTION IS THE YARDSTICK OF CHARACTER

Many people never jump into the ocean of their dreams because they feel they must have every possible answer before they leap. They ask, "What is the direction of the wind? How many seconds until the water? How many breaths to take before the plunge? What is the precise proper angle for entry? Is anyone else jumping? How many have jumped before? How many strokes to shore?"

These are reasonable questions, but some will never take the leap, no matter what the answers. Even with over-whelming evidence that the leap is safe, regardless of how many swimmers have taken the exhilarating plunge, the timid will find *something* wrong in their search, a sure sign that this leap is a doomed descent. These are those who will find a reason they cannot achieve their dreams no matter how many people around them have achieved theirs.

A pathetic majority also never cross the line between gathering information and taking action. Theirs is a life of endless contemplation, of waiting for total knowledge and perfect conditions, neither of which ever happen. Thus, they are forever destined to be observers, not masters.

Without making the actual attempt, without trial and strife, there can be no true knowledge, no progress, no high achievement, and no legend.

Those who advance do so because they value action itself. They feel that positive forward momentum—progress—is a reflection of their *character,* and so they take pride and satisfaction in actions toward that end. They think, "If I am not taking significant action to advance and progress in life, I do not feel as happy, engaged, successful, or giving." Psychologically, much is at stake based on their sense of proactivity, growth, and advancement in life. It does not mean they are ruined by failure or in the slow moments of life—it simply means they have a bias toward going and growing.

Let us remember that humankind must be measured by actions alone, not intentions. *What we intend is of little importance when judging our character or gauging our happiness.*

Only action reveals our true selves.
Only action moves us to mastery.

Only *action* allows us to create, grow, connect, contribute, rise to our highest selves, and soar into the bright stratosphere of greatness. All else is merely thought, and there is a difference between intention and initiative. Nowhere is that difference more starkly apparent than in love. We can have the *intent* to love others, but without initiative, without real acts of respect, caring, and affection for another, intention alone remains useless, soulless. *Thinking* is not love—*giving* is.

Individually, we cannot gauge who we are without looking at our actions. We do not even know what we truly value without action, because our values are more than thoughts—values are our ideals in motion, demonstrated through our interactions with others.

All that we want to feel in life—happiness, joy, satisfaction, peace, success, love—can be felt only because of our actions. We can't just think about being happy without doing something that makes us feel happiness. Imagine happiness: it is sensed only when we have done what we feel would make us happy—even if this means we simply sat down, closed our eyes, and practiced gratitude. The act of contemplating gratitude is an action generating happiness. We are joyful only if we are doing what we sense as joyful. We are satisfied only if we have done what satisfies us. We are successful only if we have done what is necessary to bring us success. We love ourselves only if we feel we deserve love by how we treat ourselves and others. Perhaps some take this too far and make doing things their only measure. But without question more people do nothing and that is why they are unhappy. Yes, we can simply focus on being, but is *being* not an action itself? Relaxing is an action. Meditating is an action. Dreaming is an action. These things bring us the emotions we desire.

Our actions are also a reliable social measure of true character. How people consistently act toward us and others gives us the data we need to judge their values, goals, and worthiness of trust and attention. Attempting to gauge someone's character with anything other than their actions is like guessing what is at the core of their hearts and minds, and guessing leads only to assumptions and drama. But action tells us what we need to know. We needn't trust a man who says he is goodwilled but has never demonstrated goodwill to another. We needn't believe the woman who says, "I love you," but then acts cruelly and without Love. When *action* is required by the moment and a person does not act, we know him to be at best lazy, and at worst a coward. Those who act cruelly are judged as cruel; those who behave idiotically are judged as fools. And so we globalize an individual's personality based on one's tendency toward advancement—those who do not advance in life are called slow, stifled, lazy, losers. Whether judgment is a good thing or a bad thing, and whether or not we are right or wrong, advancement is the yardstick we use to measure others.

Culturally, progress rides on the backs of a willful and action-driven people. Our freedoms come to us because of the actions of previous generations who strove to contribute beyond themselves. Today, the yardstick of advancement is used to gauge the health of entire societies and countries. Those who are not advanced in the areas of health, economy, technology, and freedom are seen as backward, archaic, irrelevant, the dying regimes that drift along on tradition until a mighty gust of progress destroys them.

If *positive action* is ultimately how we measure our lives, others, and our world, then let us bring it back to our daily consciousness and goals.

Let us remember that when we take action,
an invisible force gathers all around us,
pulling in opportunities that align with our purpose,
propelling us with momentum to our freedom.

And so let us have the courage to face ourselves and ask, "Am I taking enough bold and significant actions in order to advance my life and reach my full potential? If I were unafraid and acting from my highest self, what would I be doing to move forward in life? What steps must I take *today* and *this week* to begin *dramatically* advancing my health, career, family, and purpose?"

PERMISSION IS NOT REQUIRED

Those who fail to advance in life are often immature. They are over-reliant on others for their care, happiness, and success, and so they believe that other people should help them make their choices or approve of their plans and actions. They still want Mom and Dad to point the way and give a nod of approval at each tentative step. They want their teachers to give them smiles and stars. They want their lovers and friends, their bosses and coworkers, their church and their culture, to approve of their actions and be their constant cheerleaders. And the moment they don't get positive support urging them on, they stop. If they don't receive some sort of permission to be themselves or chase their dreams, they do not take those actions. They are trapped by a fear of criticism or abandonment. A long look across their lives reveals a tendency to be always waiting for permission and approval from others like a teenager waiting for permission to go out. That is their eternal state of life: *waiting for the nod of others*.

Great men and women don't give a damn if anyone approves.

They rarely seek permission from the world,
because they know that the masses bound by mediocrity
will never approve of anything that breaks convention
or smacks of boldness and magic.

They know that society has an abiding mistrust of mavericks—only, of course, until the maverick gathers abundance, power, and prestige. The great are clear with people about what they want and why, and if others criticize or judge their ideas, they take any useful feedback, discard the rest, and carry on. When people get upset or ask, "Who do you think you are?," the bold answer with strength and a readiness to defend and fight for their dreams. They do not limit their vision based on how many people nod. The belief that others do not need to grant them permission is palpable in their lives. Over and over, they began tasks, projects, and initiatives without anyone's sign-off. They didn't need a certificate, a letter of approval, or a content smile from a caregiver. They *moved*.

Let us remember this sad but sure truth: the only permission ever granted by society is permission to follow its norms and traditions. No one will grant us permission to advance quickly, because they fear being left behind or made a fool for clinging to a world already fading in relevance. With this knowledge, all that we can do once we have an idea for progress is share it openly with people, consulting intelligent sources that might make our path more successful. But we mustn't forever await approval—gather information and go and go quickly.

The most common sticking point is that we all desire to gain permission from those we trust and love. What of the woman who wants to move to a new city to chase her career ambitions but faces an unsupportive spouse? As with all relationship questions, there is no easy answer. All we can hope is that, even should she compromise for a period of time, she will ultimately proceed in some way to follow her dreams. She must find a way to honor both her desires of love *and* growth.

We must anticipate that taking actions that do not meet the approval of others will bring discord. People won't like our boldness. They will call our struggles crazy. There will be sadness and resistance from some who see us moving forward without their permission, or without *them*. This is a reality that must be faced by all those who seek to realize their dreams and potential.

Will we choose other people's opinions, preferences, and approval over our true heart's desires and growth?

The answer to the question will dictate much about the emotional joy and satisfaction we sense in life.

Perhaps it is time to remember that a higher power granted us all the permission we need to follow our heart. The universe, Nature, and God gave us power. It is not our duty to give it away by letting our choices be directed by others.

ABUNDANCE IS AT HAND

There isn't enough time. There aren't enough resources. The economy is bad. No one is making it anymore. There's not enough to go around. These are the cries of those blind to the universe's abundance.

All those who have won major life victories have found that *all the resources needed to win are within,* and that most knowledge needed to succeed is acquired *after* action.

Let us join their ranks and remember these truths: We do not need more time; we need a stronger reason to act so that we use time more effectively. We do not need to await more resources; we need to act and we will find abundance comes to us. We do not need to wait for perfect conditions; we will find perfection in progress. We do not need to ask in order to receive; we need to *give* in order to receive, for in giving we are given to. We cannot timidly wait for everything to fall into our laps; we will receive only as we rise and march, for destiny turns its ear to those without fear. These truths form the mindset of readiness and abundance that is needed to advance one's life.

The successes of this world are often people who started from scratch. Although they had limited resources, they started anyway. They built businesses and careers not because they were lucky, but because they believed that everything they needed to succeed would ultimately intersect with their actions. They knew that moving forward meant attracting attention, reward, and investment. They believed in abundance.

Contrast this mindset with that of those driven by scarcity. Because they believe there is never enough, they never act. The entrepreneur who cannot see himself becoming wealthy chooses not to execute his ideas. The executive who believes the pie will always be too small refuses to mentor others because he'll be threatened if that person should ascend. The leader of a nation who fears others will take more than they will give closes her borders or limits her trade policy. With mindsets of scarcity, they make choice after choice to self-protect, to delay, to limit, to steal, to stop.

And so let the notion of scarcity leave us completely. All that we need is abundantly within, and all good things will be attracted as we act in accordance with our dreams. It is but our own vision, will, resourcefulness, and discipline that is needed to begin—these will never be in scarce supply unless we choose to abandon them.

SUCCESS IS POSITIVE AND NECESSARY

Those who advance in life do so because they view progress— and all its resultant successes, achievements, influence, and powers—as a positive and *necessary* thing. Those doomed to the sidelines of life often mistakenly believe that success, and its resultant powers, must assuredly corrupt.

This cannot be overly stated, so let us give it close attention: The doomed expect the outcomes of advancement to be *negative,* even if they are unconscious of such expectation. They secretly believe that all this struggle toward achievement must surely lead to a hell on earth where virtue cedes the field to vice, where they will have to sell out or compromise themselves. They believe that success and power must make us *rotten;* that surely friends and family must be left by the wayside as one ascends; that love of money replaces love of meaning; that success breeds selfishness; that there is never fulfillment, only the constant lust for more; that the higher one climbs, the lonelier and more miserable one becomes. They believe in hundreds of sad and misinformed ways that success must bare only bitter fruit.

From where do such opinions rise?

First, these assumptions come from an unenlightened mind blinded by scarcity and jealousy. It is sad but true: there are small-minded people among us who dislike, distrust, or hate those who succeed in life because they falsely believe that for someone to win surely someone must lose. There are also small people who truly wish ill for those who succeed simply because they don't want to be left behind or forgotten as those around them get ahead, create more wealth, or become more influential. Seeing others who are succeeding beyond them makes them terribly uncomfortable and angry. It forces them to look in the mirror and realize they may have less luck, less opportunity, or less innate talent than others. Guilt might arise as they conclude they have less drive, discipline, and resourcefulness. Then blame begins, excuses bubble up, anger boils, all leading to victimhood and disgust for those who seem happy and successful.

From such scarcity and insecurity come the severe and misguided beliefs that those who have power are necessarily evil and corrupt, and that somehow all "those" people who are more successful than we are must surely be conspiring to hold us down. Those blinded by these assumptions cannot see their own responsibility for their reality, nor the opportunities available to all people.

This is not to say that there are not some powerful forces in the world that are oppressive, such as political tyranny, financial corruption, and the irresponsible wielding of power. But even in such extremes, we must be responsible for our reactions against such unfairness, and responsible for our ambitions and actions beyond such rare realities. Regardless of any kind of suppression, should we not still own our lives, strive hard, fight, and seek without delay our own Personal Freedom? Are there not millions of stories of men and women who came from nothing, climbed above their circumstances, broke the ceilings, became captains of their fates, and crossed impossible seas despite all obstacles? Tyranny and evil are not excuses to limit our vision for our lives.

We must be very careful. Believing, in any form, that all those who have success and power are wicked, untrustworthy, hated—and that we ourselves would become bad if we had the same success and power—is desperate, ignorant, and danger- ous. These thoughts destroy our motivation and progress in life.

First, those who *hate* successful people as a group often do so from spite, not cause, *for hatred can never have reason.* Most who hate anyone, for that matter, usually do so out of ignorant prejudices born of fearful beliefs, rather than from any real experience with those they hate. *It is a curious fact that those who hate successful people do not know many successful people.*

Our beliefs about success and wealth determine what we will pursue in life, and so we must be conscious. If we think success and power corrupt, our mind will not allow us to take action toward those things and soon we will find ourselves trapped in a life of apathy and indifference. For how could we ever be successful if we dislike the very idea of success?

The man who believes the home he is building
may house the devil someday will soon put away his tools.

To anticipate that we will become bad if we succeed, or to hate those who have succeeded is a dastardly form of self-oppression, for it confines the hater to squalor. But what of the real tyrants and discriminators who hold us back, those who cause us pain when we try to move forward, those who prejudice against us because of our race, religion, gender, lifestyle, background? *To these bastards, we owe nothing.* Our only recourse is even greater *action* toward our Personal Freedom in spite of them. Leave them, go around them, outwit them, forget them—but do not halt. On the other side of them we shall celebrate by choosing to wield our own success and influence in more giving and conscious ways.

Do not let these few people blind us. The world's successful people are more good and giving than most imagine. The higher we climb in life, the more we realize just how *hard* everyone has worked to achieve anything. We might all benefit from realizing that the majority of successful people were often plagued by desperation, heartache, and poverty. Outside of the tiny few who have advanced in life without exerting any real effort, most people of influence earned their own way by discipline, struggle, and service. They broke the chains of their resentment against others and strove for their dreams, knowing no one ultimately held them back but themselves. They recognized that poverty of intelligence, morals, and courage was more crippling than lack of wealth could ever be, and so they strengthened their mind and forged their character with hard work and noble pursuits.

What have the great done with the power they earned through striving for freedom and high achievement? More good than ill. They took care of their families for generations. They built ships and schools. They laid road and rails. They hired people, enabling them to feed and educate their children and pay their mortgages. They raised their own children and enriched their communities. They gave to others and funded the causes that a wide swath of the world benefits from every day. They gave us something to believe in, to strive for, to model. Some did this by the sheer force of their desire and faith. Others started with a measure of wealth. All who sustained it embraced the values of work, progress, service, and freedom.

Perhaps it is time we completely overcome our fears and egos, our insecurities and judgments, and learn to *celebrate* those who had the character and courage required to rise up, gain abundance, and serve greatly.

Let us remember that with progress comes power and, with power, the greater possibility to enjoy life and serve others less fortunate. *We can choose to use our success to change the world.*

To be sure, people of vice will commit more vice as they accrue more power. But we must also know that people of virtue will only spread more goodness as their influence grows. So let us work hard and enjoy the fruits of our labors without regret or small-mindedness. Let us stand on the right and generous side of might, sharing our riches and our influence with those who themselves strive for great lives and great contributions. Let us never feel we need to apologize for the power we came by through sweat and discipline. Instead let us wield it against wickedness and in service to those who believe, as we do, in the glories of the growth and generosity that success affords us. Let this be our mindset and we shall have our abundance and meaning.

STRUGGLE IS TO BE EXPECTED AND HONORED

To radically advance our lives, we will no doubt endure real struggle. We mustn't complain about it or fail to anticipate it.

There was a time when striving through trial was a *virtue*. Struggle was a cherished consequence of higher ambitions; it was taught as the necessary effort of heroism and cultural advancement; it was the celebrated context in which we proved ourselves, bettered ourselves, and realized ourselves. Only there, in the depths of effort and hardship and frustration, could our weaknesses be exposed and expelled, our lives transformed, our dreams attained, our humanity advanced. Those who struggled with honor for mighty ends were not pitied but admired and remembered across the span of time.

We must remember that the power to direct our destiny comes only from a mindset that makes us willing to struggle through learning, effort, and growth.

Yet the vast majority hate the struggle required to advance. They complain with great angst that the road to independence and abundance is too hard, too inconvenient, too slow. If there is no straight and speedy line to success, the journey never begins. People don't go back to school because it will take too long. They don't exercise because the results come too slowly. They don't fight for their dreams because it would require long nights stacked on top of already busy days. Now entire generations are narrowing their vision and efforts, fearing the hardship of facing their limitations, trying new things, and developing new talents and skill sets. The outcome is a stunningly large segment of society that is overweight, uninformed, unskilled, unhappy. It's as though real effort, the kind that involves prolonged learning and arduous nights of frustration, is avoided. Any inconvenience has become a good excuse to stop progress.

One might wonder if having the patience and persistence needed to accomplish anything worthwhile has become a thing of the past. Let us hope not, for it is only by focusing on advancing our lives that we can ever reach our potential and freedom.

None of us will rise tomorrow and say, "I do not wish to advance my life." But our wishes are not what are measured at the end of tomorrow—only our actions shall speak to who we are and what we really desire. So let us rise tomorrow with minds set for advancement. Let us be bold again. In the face of any concern, we can remember that all we need is within, that fortune favors the brave, and that action alone will illuminate the next step. Let us forever strive toward something we choose as meaningful, with a conviction so pure and powerful that we advance with grand leaps. We must commit ourselves to this cause of advancement for the sake of growth and giving. *No longer shall we wait for permission, proper timing, or ease in rapidly progressing our lives.* Let us go now. We have work to do, influence to gain, service to render, power to share, freedom to achieve for our loved ones. So let us advance and begin great things. *Now.*

DECLARATION V

WE SHALL PRACTICE JOY AND GRATITUDE

———————

Gratitude bestows reverence,
allowing us to encounter everyday epiphanies,
those transcendent moments of awe that change forever
how we experience life and the world.

SARAH BAN BREATHNACH

WE HAVE BEEN GIFTED WITH A DIVINE VITALITY and the accompanying powers of will, strength, and enthusiasm. Yet where is the energized, heightened, exhilarated pulse we would expect from such a chosen and capable people? Why do we not hear more laughter and life? Where is the vibrant, mad fury and stunning passion of the fully engaged human? Where are the shining souls whose hearts beat with racing enthusiasms? Where are the magnetism and the fire? Where are the gratitude, the joy, the spark, and the charge? What happened to that miraculous life energy that brought us into existence?

It seems that a great tidal wave of cynicism and pessimism has washed ashore and drowned the dreams of our people. The emotional energy of the world is flatlining.

We can see this drained life energy in a stunning number of people's eyes and faces, in their conduct and conversations. There is no vitality, no freedom, and no positivity in their attitude. Look how their faces seem too weathered, sallow, and stern for their age. Listen to how their conversations sound quiet and resigned, like whispers from a tired, disbanding tribe. Broaden the view and notice that most of our culture's buzz and excitement comes from a mass hysteria surrounding newfound opportunities for wealth or from the manufactured lives of the celebrity elite. Ours has become a world where a tragic number of people are more fascinated by materialism and the lives of distant narcissists than by their own life experience.

Humans are not destined to be the lazy, tired, greedy, boring caricatures of gross abundance splashed before us today with such sensationalism. Sadly, from afar, it would appear that many people have become resigned, that they have given up their remarkable potential, that they are consenting to creep instead of soar, that they risk turning into a culture of slow-moving, low-aiming, negativity-spewing brats and blamers.

One by one, we are seeing so many people for whom we care get sucked into the awful whirlpool of negativity. The energy of all this is palpable, and it must be our imperative to change it.

It must be a main aim of our lives to rekindle the magic of life. We mustn't live in the darkness of our doubts, the shadows of the joyless, or the clutches of the energy vampires. Let us remember that life's purpose is to *live*—to live freely, vibrantly, joyously, madly, consciously, lovingly, enthusiastically. Our nature gives us an intrinsic charge for such a life, and it is time to fire it once more.

We are to be radiant, grateful, buoyant people basking in our blessings and striving cheerfully toward our dreams under the bright and loving sunshine of the Divine. It takes only will and conditioning to enjoy such a life. Let us make the choice to reexamine our attitude and orientation to life, to cultivate a more positive and present pulse. Let us declare: *We Shall Practice Joy and Gratitude.*

THE JEWEL OF LIFE

The greatest of human freedoms is the ability to choose, at any moment, the palette of our emotional sky. *We alone activate the very energy and emotion through which we experience life.* If we wish to feel joy and gratitude in our lives, then we must direct our beliefs and behaviors in order to accomplish that end. And we must do it constantly, with such force and repetition that those emotions become the hues of our daily attitude. This is not easy work, but let it be our mission.

*Perhaps the severest requirement of the good life is
to have the constancy of mind to maintain our joy and gratitude
even amid hardship, pain, and injustice.*

This is the requirement of self-mastery and happiness. So it rests on our shoulders to notice when we feel bored or depressed—and to force ourselves outside to engage with the world with a smile. It's up to us to appreciate our team even when a project is failing, and to be thankful for our spouse even amid conflict.

There can be no mastery of life if we cannot transform the energy we feel at any moment into cheerful engagement and deep appreciation. The self-labeled "realists" will tell us this is impossible. They, who have abandoned hope, will say that our world is too stressful and cruel, that our genetics and environment are destined to dominate our life and feelings. They will insist that our unconscious minds and reptilian impulses for fear and selfishness will rule the day no matter what we do.

But let our own minds decide what is real and what is possible for us. Let our own eyes see among the bored and battered faces a starkly different, brighter lot. There are those whose faces are so alight with life that they serve as a blinding reminder, amid the darkness of our time, that joy and charisma and hope still exist. These are the energizers, the cheerful individuals who inspire and enliven those around them *even though* their own backgrounds, genetics, and environments would give cause for them to be apathetic and detached. They, too, might have come from a broken home or poverty. But instead of choosing bitterness, they seem blissfully aware of, and deeply thankful for, their blessings, *even when* those blessings are fewer and more meager than others. These few, the energized and happy and thankful among us, are not "lucky," nor are they to be envied. For their treasures are available to all of us. Their treasure is freely chosen attitude.

We are not blind to the fact it is difficult to choose joy in an agitated, chaotic, often angry world. The social contagion of negativity spreads quickly because the human mind is susceptible. We are wired to sense and mirror the emotional energy around us. Seeing fear on someone's face can trigger a state of fear. Such emotional contagion had primitive benefits once. It was a blessing in times of grave danger. When the faces of our friends contorted in fear and they began to flee from some unseen threat, we saw their terrorized faces and automatically felt afraid and fled with them even before knowing the threat. This prevented us from being eaten or maimed by a prowling animal or murderous band of men.

But this primal protection is now a mortal enemy. Without predators on the hunt for our flesh, with little to fear but fear itself, and in a world full of bored, fearful, sullen people, this mirroring impulse can ruin our lives. The energy of the masses is, at best, a low-tier energy, an emotionally bleak space created by a confused yet cynical people operating on little sleep, high stress, and a frenetic desire to be somewhere else, with someone else, doing something else. We must ask ourselves: *Should I conform to their energy? And what of their thoughts and language?*

When the trite and bewildered cynic tells us that the world is going to hell, should we let our mind automatically seek to confirm this reality? Should we, too, allow our mind to cast around for something to complain about? Will we allow all the negative and needy energy of the world to infiltrate and spoil our motivation or serenity?

We mustn't become catastrophes of energetic conformity. We must use our consciousness to overpower our mirroring impulses. The more we automatically allow ourselves to sync with others' energy levels—unless they are the emotional energies of joy, love, and enthusiasm we ourselves wish to feel—the more we diminish our personal power. The more often we fall in line with the poor language and attitude of the drowning masses, the more we sound and look like victims. We must never forget that ours is a world of distracted people craving Personal Freedom but often choosing to operate from fear. And so if we aren't conscious with our will and vigilance, we risk sliding into their tragedy. *Life can lose its vibrant aura and charm if we do not bend the energy of our minds toward positive engagement and appreciation.* And so let us take back our focus and remember the riches: joy is the jewel of life, gratitude the gold.

THE JOYOUS MASTER

What is the magic of the joyous few who illuminate the world? Where do they find such pleasure in life, and how do they exude such positivity?

Theirs is a simple formula. The joyous are simply more conscious and consistent in their attempts to sense and generate joy and gratitude. They try harder, making joy a practice, a habit, a consistent condition of their character, an enduring social art amid glum and boring times.

They have made it their aim to live a joyous life. That is all.

No smoke, no mirrors. Just those simple forces at work that sustain motivation: attention and effort toward that which they desire.

This answer is not popular. It isn't easy to admit that we do not try often or hard enough. But if joy is lacking in our lives, we must accept the clear truth that we are not often enough bending our will to joy. We can lie and say that joyful people have it easier than we do. But we all know happy people who have less fortune and health than we.

Let us look to the instruction of those little happy people around us. Children have joy naturally. Their curiosity, lack of expectations, pleasure in small things, and full engagement in the moment are quick-sprouting seeds of joy. We can learn from them. What would happen if we put their natural inclinations for joy into our lives? Could we shift to being more curious about our immediate surroundings? Won't releasing expectation, especially the expectation that perfection should surround us everywhere we go, bring new delights? Can we take pleasure in small things and expecting good things to come our way? Surely, doing these things would change our lives.

Let us return then to the instruction of happy children again and again: *Be curious. Release expectation. Take pleasure in small things and expect good things. Cheerfully engage the moment.* Let this become our practice, our mastery, and our art.

Those who perfect bringing joy to every day of their lives are not unlike any other master—they work so hard at something that it soon becomes *play*. The greatest artists and athletes, the highest-achieving executives and entrepreneurs, the happiest laborers and the most respected leaders all lose themselves in their work with great zeal and enthusiasm. Their efforts are like a game. They immerse themselves cheerfully as if playing to their strengths in a grand sandlot. They do not look angry, bewildered, frustrated, or restless but rather relaxed, effortless. Even in chaos and turmoil, they meet struggle with intense and spirited joy. They engage in the challenge and honor it as if they expected it and accept it. Even amid the discomfort of growing complexity of building their lives and their careers, they often appear unfazed and nearly serene. They often sing while they toil, and smile when perplexed and working. They spend and stretch themselves with devotion, willing themselves to remain positive and cheerful, knowing that one day their diligence will make them masters, knowing that one day they will have their victory and transcendence. *These are the joyous masters.*

The joyous masters know that struggle does not always have to equal suffering. Let us learn from them and remember there can be joy and spirit in meeting life's demands, in stretching beyond comfort, in pushing through times of high exertion and low achievement.

The joyous masters know that life is a journey, a trying and exciting adventure whose destination matters less than the passion and freedom felt along the way. Let us learn from them and remember that, even when we are weary or uncertain, we can feel presence and eagerness for each moment.

The joyous masters know that amid all the chaos and conflict, all the hurry and wickedness of the world, *there is something solid within that is beautiful and steady and good.* Like them, we can have the sense that our mind and soul are fresh and pure and clean, even as we slug it out in the thick mess of humanity.

The joyous masters know that nothing good comes easily, but that all things can be met with peace. Like them, we can show grace even in the tightening grip of pain, and face our long trials with serenity and dignity and enthusiasm for a new day.

The joyous master knows that, in time, everyone will find their path, so the ultimate virtues are patience and Love. Like them, we can know that there is no need to force or coerce others into our quest or joys. No matter how unwilling or undirected someone appears in this moment or this year, we know that all will find their way eventually to their own sense of freedom.

Let us pray that we may find the will and strength to learn such things, to practice such things, to become such masters.

THE PATH OF GRATITUDE

We should not focus on the shadow in the corner and be so foolish as to miss the fact that the shadow exists only because the room is illuminated. There is light all around, there is much to be grateful for in this seemingly dark world, and so all we must do is pull our gaze from the shadow and look to the ocean of divine light and grace in which we are blessed to live.

To the attuned and grateful, the cascade of the universe's blessings feels like a magnificent waterfall of luck and wonder. In searching for things to be grateful for, we need not look far. One must simply release the ego, let down the persona that feels it has created all things or must perfect all things, and accept the natural, the unexplainable, the energy that has graced us with vitality and a world of magic.

A vibrant and happy life begins at the path of gratitude.

So let us be more appreciative and thankful each day:

Let me be thankful for all the light that surrounds me.

Let me be thankful to any caregivers who inspire me.

Let me be thankful to my lover, who overlooks my shortcomings.

Let me be thankful to the women and men who risk their lives to protect my freedoms.

Let me be thankful for the blue tint of the sky and the beauty of our natural world.

Let me be thankful for the heart that drums life through me.

Let me be thankful for last night's rest, no matter its length.

Let me be thankful for my gifts of free will, of volition, of endurance.

Let me be thankful to my mentors and to the traitors who also instructed me.

Let me be thankful that I am not living in deeper need and squalor.

Let me be thankful for my home, for my daily bread, for my clean water.

Let me be thankful for the opportunity to work and create and earn.

Let me be thankful for the luck that has advanced me, and the disasters and tribulations that have educated me.

Let me be thankful for the blank slate that comes with each morning.

Let me be thankful for my breath and the clean moment at hand.

Let me be thankful to my Creator.

It is in finding so many things to be thankful for that we become appreciative and *alive*. Just as we have done with joy, let us make it our aim to become masters of gratitude.

WE ARE BLESSED

How shall we maintain so much joy and gratitude in our lives?

We remember always that our emotional state is a choice, a selection from a broad palate of reactions and feelings available to us at any moment. As a power plant does not have energy but generates energy, we do not *have* happiness, we create it, generate it, and transform lower energies into higher energies. Similarly, we do not *have* joy or gratitude—we generate and experience them by our will.

We can make joy and gratitude a daily habit and standard simply by measuring how often we cultivate such emotions. Several times each day we can assess our success by asking, *"On a scale of 1 to 10, how much joy and gratitude am I bringing to this moment?"*

There is power in this wording. We are not asking how much joy and gratitude we are *experiencing* in the moment, as if we are somehow entitled to such high emotions. We are demanding personal responsibility—how much am *I bringing?*

In rating our emotional reality, we become more aware and we allow our mind to decide if the answer is acceptable based on the quality of life we desire. If we are living at low levels of joy and gratitude, our intuitive nature will demand that we heighten our focus and emotion. Perhaps we might be thankful for the self-reproach that stirs our minds and souls to higher levels of energy when we know we could be happier and more grateful. Yes, let us be thankful for that, and for all things, for we are blessed.

Declaration VI

WE SHALL NOT
BREAK INTEGRITY

First say to yourself what you would be;
and then do what you have to do.

EPICTETUS

I N OUR DARKEST HOURS, WE ARE TEMPTED TO BREAK
our integrity—to compromise who we are, what we
believe in, and what we know to be right and true and good.
There is an opportunity to be weak and heartless, and it is
taken. An impulse arises to be cruel or to cheat or to run from
our very own dreams, and it is sadly followed. Right when it
counts the most, we forget what is important and abandon our
higher moral convictions. We make an important promise to
our children or team but don't follow through. We lash out
in anger at those we love when they are most vulnerable. We
lie to someone we care about even though we absolutely know
they are desperate to hear the truth. We let disappointment win
the day and hastily quit on our dreams just because we stum-
bled and fell and made a mess of ourselves. We withhold

our voice when we have a chance to shine, hiding our true selves at the expense of authenticity and growth. We act indifferent or cowardly just when the world needs our presence and strength. These are moments when we experience a sudden rupture of mind and spirit, a lack of virtue, a descent into the dark planes of selfishness and irresponsibility.

Perhaps it is not always so dramatic. Not all compromises of our character are, like the movies often portray, centered on huge and vexing life decisions. There is no tearing out of hair as we desperately try to figure out what to do, as if a grand existential dilemma is unfolding all around. There is no dramatic debate in a public square or a conflict so heated someone collapses to the ground because they can't stand to give an inch. No, most breaks in our integrity are small in scale and go unnoticed. They often come when we are too busy to pay attention. We didn't even notice we were rude. We didn't realize it became a habit to act unlike ourselves, to tell little lies, to be easily angered, to keep our ideas to ourselves, to talk too much about ourselves, to gossip, to delay, to ridicule, to be late, to forget the thank-you's and the I-love-you's. We broke stride with who we are and how we want others to perceive us because of little throwaway acts that we didn't realize were solidifying into a character that was, likely, beneath us.

It is time to remind ourselves that today's thoughts and actions become our legacy. When we forget this or lie to ourselves thinking our actions do not matter, we have permission to act as momentary buffoons. We let ourselves break, just this once, from our values. We cheat, just this once. We lie, just this once. We put off the hard task, just this once. We skip the workout, just this week. We take the drink, just one more. And soon we find that each of these little breaks in our will leads to another, and then to a lifetime of compromise and regret. Without vigilance, what is right and strong about the human spirit can be whittled away and broken forever.

Let us not forget that our actions form, piece by piece, a structure that is either upright or crooked. And so let us aim to be our highest selves, keeping our character and values intact, meeting every situation with solid integrity and generous humanity. When the next temptation comes to be weak and heartless—and it will come—we will not take it. Instead there will be a strong, grounded refusal to break, a decision not to compromise or lower ourselves, that mighty lift that comes from doing what's right, a grand ascent to another realm of human character when we are congruent with our divine nature.

Personal Freedom, and the hope of mankind, rests on our commitment to stay true to ourselves, our dreams, our word, our goodness, and our loving nature. By refusing to bend on our values, *we* become unbreakable—solid and stable, courageous and certain, men and women of valor, worth, and character. Let us build a life we are proud of. Let us declare: *We Shall Not Break Integrity.*

CREATING CLARITY

When we are incongruent, acting in ways that are not aligned with our beliefs, we feel "off," frustrated, regretful, and, over time, miserable. But when we align our thoughts and actions with our values and priorities in life, we enjoy the blessings of a chosen and satisfying life. This knowledge requires us to ask two questions: *Who am I, and what is important to me?* These contemplations may be two of the most important in life. No profound personal power or full freedom can belong to those who do not know the answers.

To find our answer to such daunting questions, it is helpful to consider the qualities we desire in three separate areas of our lives: our character, our connections, and our contributions.

On Character

Very few people have ever done deep work in defining their character—the specific identity they wish to have. They simply respond to the world on a whim, without paying any real attention to the type of person they want to be or become. With no targeted identity to act toward, they become amalgamations of the desires of others and the circumstances and cultures in which they live. They have no real character because they are slave to impulse and mimicry.

Contrast this with a woman who owns keen self-awareness. If she is vitally aware and committed to being a kind person, she is rarely rude. If she has defined herself as deeply empathetic, she intentionally develops the discipline to listen more, to help more, and to love more. She works to align all her thoughts and habits with the ideal person she wishes to be. *Awareness and discipline give her freedom to live her potential.*

Do we have this level of self-mastery? Do we know what qualities of character would make us feel congruent, happy, and whole? If not, let us ask, "If I were to die tomorrow, how would I want others to remember me? What exact words and phrases would I be happy to hear them use to describe me? When I guide my decisions and actions today, what exact words and phrases should penetrate my mind and inspire me to be a good human?" The answers to these questions give us focus in life. Should we desire to be remembered as vibrant, kind, intelligent, loving, and courageous, then we can choose to live in alignment with those descriptions.

To some, this seems too basic a premise. But common sense is not always common practice.

How many times have we caused ourselves pain
because we failed to pause and think,
"How would my best self view and respond to this situation?"

This must be our day to define the best of who we are and what we will stand for. Tonight, in the glow of gratitude for our free will, let us write down the words and phrases that describe our ideal identity. Put them on beautiful paper and in ink. Carry them everywhere. Look at these words, memorize them, verbalize them—*become* them. The more we align our actions with this identity, the more free, motivated, and whole we shall become. Life will feel brighter and more our own, more deep and satisfying. Destiny will smile on us and we will be welcomed into the gates of heaven as people of purpose and integrity.

On Connection

Let us also define how we shall interact with the world. What kind of experiences do we want to have with the important people in our lives?

Those who fail to consider this always fail in their relationships. Imagine the man who has no clarity or commitment for the quality of interactions he has with his wife. If she is upset, he is likely to simply mirror her feelings and frustrations. But he should say to himself, "I will be a present, stable, and solid husband for my wife, and this means I will be alert and attentive to her feelings. I will listen to her closely, and I will seek to be empathetic and supportive, even in times of crisis or conflict." He can go to an even greater specificity in his interactions with her, thinking of how he would like to connect with her while out to dinner, during their commute to work, on their vacations, at times when they are challenged with their finances or their children. The more thoughtful he is *in advance* of these situations, the more intentional and consistent he becomes during them. His integrity is made public and real, and soon he will be proud of—and loved for—his actions.

We should sit and write these things out: *Who is important to me and why? How shall I interact with them so that they are appreciated and experience the best of who I am? What kind of person should I become so that I am happy with how I treat others?* Tomorrow, then, let us rise to give our full effort to being that kind of person and interacting with others as we desire. If we can do this each day of our life, then when our final hours greet us we shall be surrounded by those we love and serve, and they shall tell us *why* they loved us, and a wide smile shall spread across our face knowing that their descriptions reveal something important—that we lived and loved in congruence with our heart and highest humanity.

On Contribution

Finally, let us define the contributions we wish to make. What do we want to create, build, shape, share, or give? Beyond our interactions with people, what things do we wish to give them or leave them? What tangible evidence of our creativity and life do we want to leave on this earth?

Too many people are failing to think of these questions, and so they are bartering away their integrity day by day in unfulfilling tasks. They are not working toward something real and meaningful, something they know will bring them joy and fulfillment. They say yes to too many projects in order to please others, at the cost of their own satisfaction and soul. Had they been proactive in defining what is meaningful and important to them, they could have avoided feeling so distracted and unfulfilled. There is no reason for us to suffer their same fate now. Let us sit down, pen in hand once more, and describe the projects and aims that give us energy, enthusiasm, and meaning. We have written these things before, but in writing them we reconnect to our motivation and our power. So, what will we be proud to contribute to and accomplish in life? What service will we provide? What art will we create and leave behind? What difference will we make? From such questions is birthed a life that matters. But without vision into these things, we have nothing to align ourselves to. *Where there is no clarity, there can be no integrity.*

Armed with intentions for who we wish to be, how we wish to interact with others, and what we wish to give, we become conscious people. We gain the full might of our personal power.

THE SIX PRACTICES OF INTEGRITY

Wisdom is knowing who to be and what to do in a given situation; virtue is acting on that wisdom. We all know that we should be thoughtful, kind, loving, and happy people, yet not all of us choose to be those things. This chasm between knowing and doing is the dark pit where people lose themselves. Every violation against our values and virtue is a slice against our integrity and happiness. But every stand we make to express our integrity is another brick added to the great structure of character we are erecting each day.

And so let us choose wise life practices. The first practice of integrity is to *think before we act*. No major decision or action should be made without considering the major categories of our life: our personal well-being, our relationships, and our social responsibilities. We must ask, "Are the choices I am about to make going to support my sanity and happiness as well as the health and welfare of my family and community? What would happen if my choices and actions were broadcast on the evening news—would I be proud of them?" Failing to ask such questions has led many good people to descend into bad ones.

The second practice of integrity is to *never commit to anything where we lack passion*. We must stop saying yes to everything, as many of our failures occurred because we began something with half-heartedness. As we become more mature and enlightened adults, we come to realize that if an opportunity is presented to us and it does not gain a near 100-percent enthusiasm and commitment from us, then the reply must be a 100-percent *no*. Often, breaking integrity means repeatedly doing things we do not love with people we do not care for. Isn't life meant to be a passionate love affair with our work, our faith, and those we are blessed to know, care for, and serve? Then let us maintain that passion through spending our time wisely.

The third practice is to *keep our word*. If we say we will meet our lover at noon, then we must arrive at or before noon. When we promise to complete the project by Wednesday, then we shall turn it in on Wednesday. Should we tell another we will keep their confidence, then we must not gossip. This practice is one of the highest arts of life: to remain true and noble and trustworthy. Imagine completing our life and saying, "I was a person that people could count on. I showed up when I said I would. I gave what I said I would. I delivered because I cared for my integrity and the people in my life." We ought to pray we can live such a life, and we should complement those prayers with action to make it so.

The fourth practice is to *always treat others with respect.* Those reflecting on their lives often regret that they treated people poorly. Almost all suffering in our personal relationships comes from a lack of respect given to or from others. But few people have a clear definition of what respecting another means. Giving respect means to do no harm; to allow others their rights in expressing themselves; and to honor the fact that their own thoughts, feelings, and actions are real and justifiable in their own minds, even if we see them as unimportant or wrong. Respect does not necessarily mean approval; one can respect another's right to speak but not necessarily approve of what is spoken. Respect means that we see others as doing their best with what they have, who they are, and what hand they've been dealt, even if we find their efforts wanting in any way. It means seeing the divinity in others, and never inviting disrespect into our lives by projecting disrespect onto others.

The fifth practice is to *tell the truth*. How much trouble do we get into by lying? How many of our big upsets or strained relationships are amplified by a small fib? The woman who tells many lies is forced to live many lives, thus lacking a singular character and mind. The man who lies today is haunted tomorrow, doomed until the specter of his very own lie appears in front of all, at which time he will be preoccupied by the judgments of others. Internally and externally he is guaranteed only pain. To lie to oneself or to others, then, is to wound oneself. We mustn't allow ourselves the temporary ease of telling any lie; the long-term cost is always embarrassment and regret. We must not chip away at our integrity one small lie at a time.

The sixth practice is to *always favor action*. If we stand doubtful and delayed on the sidelines of life, it as if we stood at the edge of a river and did not wade in to save a drowning child. When we see a beautiful woman and desire to speak with her but do not approach, regret will follow us. Should we dream of beginning a new career but never take action, regret will ultimately consume us. When our mind wants something for good and meaningful reasons and we do not pursue it, this is like dismissing our own self. The less we act, the less integrity we have with our own heart and mind. The less we trust ourselves, know ourselves, love ourselves. So let us remember that integrity is found in taking actions that support our genuine desires and values.

None of these six practices require anything extraordinary—they are all natural impulses. But it is our day-to-day failures in maintaining them that cause most of our human suffering. The more of these practices we enact, the more we experience human happiness.

Why do we universally admire and respect a Gandhi, Mandela, Mother Teresa, Lincoln, or any other leader or legend from history's pantheon? It is because they were guided by these integrity-based practices. They stood for something. They didn't break with the values they believed in just because they faced struggle. They were good people who kept integrity between their words and actions. We can follow their lead. We can become people who are strong and proud and respectable. All we must do is make integrity a lifelong *practice*.

THE SEVEN TEMPTATIONS

And so let us anticipate the situations in life that are most likely to cause us to break our integrity. In a stunning lack of self-knowledge, people are often surprised that certain circumstances cause them to react in ways that are beneath them. It's as though they never paid attention to when other people became angry or unhappy, and thus never learned how to avoid becoming angry or unhappy. They have been stupid to the lessons of the world, and so they regularly behave stupidly.

Perhaps it is time to review what we have learned from the wisdom of the sages and our own experience. By now, we should all know that we can easily lose integrity when we are feeling or reacting to any of these things: *impatience, disappointment, desperation, aggression, hurt, loyalty,* and *power.* Those are the Seven Temptations. Let us know them well so we can prepare for them and remain true to our highest selves when faced with them.

The Temptation of Impatience

We begin with *impatience.* At some point in our lives, we have all lost ourselves when our patience was tested. Even if we view ourselves as a kind and loving parent, when the kids ignore our fifth request to quiet down, it is easy to explode in anger. Should our new business not succeed as fast as we wish, it is easy to quit the pursuit of our dream.

Lack of patience has made many good men mean, scores of would-be successes failures, and countless good ideas abandoned just as they were about to become real. It has also led to almost all cultural ills related to greed and poor financial decision-making—this despicable focus on short-term profit rather than long-term growth.

Free and conscious people develop a high degree of emotional intelligence that alerts them when they become too hurried, impatient, or irritable. Through practice and discipline, they condition their mind to issue an early warning system that says, "I am panicked and likely to make a bad decision. I must take a breath and slow down. It would be more intelligent and responsible to calm down now, to overcome the stress of this moment, and then do what is right for the long term."

We can begin to develop this skill by reflecting on times we were impatient: "When was the last time I lashed out at a loved one because of my inability to keep patience and perspective? What could I have done better in that situation to calm myself? What other situations seem to infuriate me with impatience over and over again? How will I choose to respond in those situations in the future?" The more we reflect on the times when our impatience got the better of us, the less likely we are to repeat our failures of character.

When we look to our future, let us imagine how we wish to be remembered. The good parent wants their children to say, "My parent was patient and loving with me." The good businessperson wants their employees to say, "I am glad our founder stuck through the hardship and kept their vision alive rather than quit too soon."

Nothing here should surprise us. The wise have always taught, "Patience is a virtue." To keep our integrity in life, let us make that commonsense common practice.

The Temptation of Disappointment

Many people break from their integrity because of disappointment. Things don't turn out as they desire and their ego flames and fumes, causing them to break commitments to themselves and others. This is the woman who tries a new weight loss program and gets results, but because she hasn't lost *as much* weight as she anticipated, she breaks her resolutions and goes back to old habits. It's the workingman who promises to work harder, but upon seeing his first efforts go unnoticed, he quickly drifts back into mediocrity. It's the entrepreneur whose first attempt ends in failure, so he decides to go back to a joyless job for a better sense of security.

For most, disappointment isn't the problem; it's what they do after they feel disappointment—they *quit*. Disappointment is just the excuse small people use to justify their urge to quit and to enjoy a life of ease over the hard work and trial necessary for real achievements.

More conscious people see disappointment as a common and harmless reality of having high aims and standards. *If we are not disappointed from time to time, we are not attempting anything new or bold or significant.* So let us realize disappointment is necessary and holds no real power over us. In truth, disappointment often dies when we adopt a learning mindset. Rather than being saddened or frustrated to a point of failure, we must simply become curious, asking, "What can I learn here that will help me alter my approach? What lessons must I understand so that next time I can be even more of my best self and provide even more of my best service to the world?"

The contrast could be no less stark. Unsuccessful people allow disappointment to stop them in their tracks, to break from their commitments and values and dreams. They let disappointment grow into an *identity* of failure. Successful people feel disappointment and *learn through it and let it go.* They use disappointment to enlarge their competency, not let it cut their character or fell their dreams. A disappointed failure or a learning achiever? Let us choose this day, once and for all, which group we shall belong to.

The Temptation of Desperation

The most predictable moments when people break their integrity are when they are desperate, on the brink of ruin. The businessperson nearing bankruptcy decides to do something dishonest to make a fast but dirty buck. The person starving for love compromises herself to gain acceptance and affection. The student desperate to live up to others' expectations cheats on test after test. The hungry man steals sustenance.

We have all made bad decisions when we were needy. So let us remember them and look for patterns: What point of need drove us to bad behavior? How did we think about others, the world, and ourselves in those unhealthy or irresponsible moments? How could we have behaved differently—in ways that would have supported our faster rise and a higher sense of integrity? What are we committed to in similar situations in the future?

We would be fools not to anticipate that desperation will greet us again in the future if we are pursuing our dreams. We will get knocked down. We will struggle and we will likely at some point lose money, status, and influence. We will be forced to scrape together every ounce of our resources and respect to continue on. And so let us decide *now* how we will behave in those moments.

In every great story there is always a scene when the central character becomes desperate and afraid. How they behave in the moments afterward dictates whether or not they are cowards, villains, or people of integrity and valor who save the day and ride proudly into the bright horizon. When our hour arrives, when we suddenly fall into a pit of need, let us act in accordance of our highest values and show the world just what we're made of.

The Temptation of Aggression

People are often at their absolute worst when responding to others' aggression. If they are bullied, they become violent. If their spouse is pushing an idea that they dislike, they fly into a rage. If their boss tells them firmly what to do, they weaken and agree to it, even when they disagree with all their soul. Yet our goal should never be to meet someone's assertiveness with an action that makes us small, angry, or hurtful. No good comes from becoming bitter or violent.

When others are aggressive, that is the time to be hyperaware of our reactions. When others push too hard, let us simply accept they are acting from a place of ego and often ignorance, and direct our own mind to not lower ourselves to their level. That is when we should ask, "If I removed my anger or hurt from this situation and acted from my highest self, what would I do now?" Responding well to such a question is what made Gandhi and King and Mandela so focused and true and admired.

The world will push at us and enervate us and seek our conformity and obedience. People will be rude and mean and absentminded. So let us choose a higher road, maintaining our values and standing for peace even in the midst of what feels like war. Over time, we will always find that patience shall overcome aggression and Love shall overcome hate.

The Temptation of Hurt

Vigilance is also required when we are hurt or experiencing *any* negative emotion. Otherwise we can become the woman who feels wronged and becomes spiteful, even though she does not see herself as a spiteful human; the man who physically attacks another person because a verbal insult made him feel small; the leader who decides to derail an entire project because he was embarrassed.

This an area in need of examination. Let us ask, "How do I usually act when I am hurt? How do I see and react to other people when I am in a negative mood? What reminders can I give myself the next time I am feeling hurt so that I stay true to myself and keep progressing in life?"

Maturity insists we recognize that feeling hurt requires the same thing as feeling happy: a conscious *choice.* When a hurt wells up in our heart, let us examine whether or not it useful to keep around. Let us realize it is our own internal representation of a situation that we alone have given meaning to. We can feel the hurt, but we must release it quickly and never aim it at others. *Integrity is learning to feel hurt but not integrate its darkness into our soul or cast it onto another.*

The Temptation of Loyalty

Not all breaks from our integrity are for self-protection or want of character. Often, we break from what we know is right out of *good intentions.* It is an odd truth that the liars among us are most often good and loyal people who lie in order to *protect* someone they love or respect. This is the man who believes himself a good husband and lies to his wife in order not to hurt her, the supposed good friend who doesn't want to expose her girlfriend who has been having an affair, the leader who withholds information to protect his company's reputation.

But when loyalty is chosen over truth, corruption is always near. Small lies to protect those we love, work with, or care for become bigger lies. If we lie for others, an "us against them" mentality develops, in which we mistakenly pit them and us against the world, failing to recognize that our lies hurt other people. We justify lies as if blind to their inevitable ripple effect of hurt.

Must we never lie? What else could be our aim? Any other intention is to willingly sully our soul. Should we find ourselves in a moment in which we feel we must lie to absolutely ensure the safety or health of ourselves or another, we should still be cautious. We often believe total disaster will befall our lives if we should tell the truth, and this is most often untrue itself. There is a reason all spiritual texts say in some form or another that the truth shall set us free. If our or our loved one's backs are truly against the wall and definite harm will occur if we speak the truth, then the best we can do is favor silence over false words. We can speak up in honesty for those we love but we need not speak in falsehoods to protect their irresponsible behaviors. We needn't choose to forfeit our character simply because someone else's has been compromised.

Should we wish a pure and clean spirit, let us be cautious against all practices or justifications of lying. This is not an easy practice, but a life of disingenuous ease is not what we are after. The path to transcendence is illuminated by truth.

The Temptation of Power

Power itself is not bad; it is the means by which some people seek or wield it that can cause harm. On the way to power, people who lack integrity and virtue lie, cheat, steal, and step on others. But likewise those who maintain virtue use their power to advance good ideas and lift up people in need.

The secret to seeking power with integrity is to stop imagining that when we finally have it, we will suddenly *change*. The evil person will only become more evil with greater power. The kind person, kinder. The loving, more loving. The generous, more generous. As we seek more money or influence, let us be clear about who we are today, knowing that this will simply be amplified when we gain power. And so let us write some more: "When I gain more influence through wealth or status or luck, what shall I do with it so that I remain true and proud of who I am?"

In acquiring abundance and influence we must remain true to what we stand for and the best of who we are each and every day of our lives. *That* is real power.

ACTION BECOMES CHARACTER

Our actions are creating a character that will stand tall or shrink into the darkness of regret. To be wise and virtuous humans, then, conscientiousness is required, especially when faced with the Seven Temptations of impatience, disappointment, desperation, aggression, hurt, loyalty, and power.

The world will constantly bombard us with opportunities to be small and catty people. It would be easy to give up on ourselves and our dreams. It would be easy to treat others poorly. But that is not our path. Freedom and victory belong to those who remain strong and true despite temptation.

Declaration VII

WE SHALL
AMPLIFY LOVE

Someday, after mastering the winds,
the waves, the tides and gravity,
we shall harness for God the energies of love, and then,
for a second time in the history of the world,
man will have discovered fire.

PIERRE TEILHARD DE CHARDIN

THERE IS NO BEAUTY IN THE WORLD MORE PERFECT, more awe-inspiring, more human and transfixing than unfiltered, unashamed love. We are at our finest when we give and live in love, and at our worst when we hoard it, deny it, or choke it out of existence. Love, like nothing else, can make us soar to our highest heights or suffer our deepest lows. In the moments defined by the presence of love, we touch the face of our highest self and of the Divine. To stand emotionally open before the world and give of our hearts without fear of hurt, attachment, or demand of reciprocity—this is the ultimate act of human courage, this the ultimate experience of Personal Freedom.

Love is our origin and our final destination. Our spirit was animated by the loving energy of a higher power, and as we release our last breath our spirits will dissipate back into that love.

With love's transcendent power, we can be reborn and redirected. When we open to it, life itself can feel newer, more alive, more magical and meaningful. When we ready ourselves for our ultimate destiny, when we release our childish, selfish needs and realign our priorities to those of the heart, we can finally reach those magnificent fields of human empathy, kindness, compassion, forgiveness, generosity, and courage.

We must stop pretending that there is not enough love in the world to give or receive, as though love can somehow be diminished or squandered by human force. Love is a divine energy, always present, accessible, flowing. If we accept this much, we can go further. We can let go of past hurts, for they have nothing to do with the reality of love itself. And we can stop playing our petty games, slowly pacing the release of our love to the world only when it feels safe. Limiting how much love we give to others because we fear lack is an act of cowardice, not divine strength. And so let us now sense love anew, from a different, divine perspective. Let us feel its abundance and let it emanate through us in its full force so that we might soar and serve at levels beyond human imagination. Let us declare: *We Shall Amplify Love.*

LIFE'S ANIMATING ENERGY

The desire to love and be loved is one of our most animating energies. All of our desires, all of our meaningful hopes and dreams, rest on and return again and again to love. Nothing remarkable in our personal growth can be achieved without opening to love and unleashing its joyful fire into the world. Life's greatest victories are won on the fields of love. Yet we often block this divine energy. Look to our long line of failures in matters of the heart:

the hurt and miserable souls, torn by sorrow,
who haven't the courage to love again;
the morose masses who have resigned themselves to the
myth that there is nothing left to feel, no new level of love
to activate or draw from in their relationships;
the broken thugs who take the lives of others because
they lack the courage to give or ask for more love;
the oblivious leaders who cannot grasp that
caring and compassion are their best tools
for shaping people's hearts and minds;
the sad wanderers who have caged their hearts
from others yet who prostitute themselves to feel connected
and accepted in some way, to have a tiny sense
of the part they have so fearfully locked away,
the passionless marriages and the doubtful lovers,
the bitter and broken who feel that love was stripped away
and forever stolen from them;
the pacing and metering of how we release love,
as if it were a finite resource that could be used up.

Look closer still, to how we tune out the better angels of our nature and ignore our loved one's request for us to be more present, caring, and empathetic—someone more loving.

How do we not become hardened by such gross heartache and neglect?

We begin by recasting our conception of love itself. Despite yesterday's tragedy or today's pain, we must sense and amplify love anew, this time with more of us in play, this time with *greater force and depth.*

Surely, we are aware that more love is in itself a good thing, that opening ourselves more to love is akin to opening life's secret treasures, that more love makes us more empathetic, connected, and influential with others. Love is a practical tool for bettering our lives. If we are loving to those around us, then we create the conditions for a positive environment and deeply fulfilling emotional and social life. Let us make that our aim.

THE CLOSING OF THE HEART

Why is love so tragically absent from so many lives? Why is the courage to love openly, faithfully, and without measure such a feared premise?

It began with hurt.

We were born a vessel flowing with authentic and abundant love. Then things changed. We weren't cared for the way we might have been. We didn't get the attention we craved. Someone pointed at us, judged us, ridiculed us, rejected us. Callous words and selfish acts left us sad and scared. We were burned, crushed, embarrassed, shamed, or smothered by cruel intentions and warped forms of selfish love. And so we began the long, steady, hard work of closing off our hearts, protecting our soul's light, building a high wall around what we are capable of feeling and giving.

Soon, we allowed only a few people, those we deemed safe, to peer above this thick, cold, impenetrable wall. And even to those chosen few we offered only piecemeal glimpses of what we really had to give, measuring out how much we would show them, how much we would allow our hearts to light up for them, when and if at all we would give ourselves permission to say life's three most important words.

It is how it goes:
We measure out the giving and receiving of love,
and it makes us suffer so.

Over time the wall of protection has become so impervious and so forbidding that it has blocked out the one thing the wall was built to protect: love.

The tragedy of humanity's great walling off of love is that the construction began and was laid haphazardly, in fits and starts and terrible spurts of immature confusion. By the time we hit adolescence, we became driven by a mass hysteria that said "protect your heart," and we began to believe, falsely, that love *itself* had enemies. We let the slings and arrows from others hit our heart, and we felt that love was somehow diminished or damaged. We were swept into a collective unconsciousness that believes that hurt has something or anything to do with love at all, and for this too many have drowned in needless misery.

Hurt has nothing to do with love, and love is unaffiliated with and unaffected by pain. We say, *"My heart is full of love,"* but love is not bound in our heart or our relationships, and thus, it is not caged and capable of being poked, taunted, or trapped. And no amount of love—no matter the pain or hurt—is ever "lost."

Love is not confined to the human heart and, thus, cannot be held in or out. It is our lack of this awareness that has made us at first seek to protect love and then to limit its release with such fear. We believe it to be a finite thing that we own and can lose. We think it is scarce, delicate. But we are wrong, and this fallacy is what makes life lose its color, what rips away the joy, connection, and sacredness of life.

TRUE DIVINITY

Love is divine. It is a spiritual energy that is, at this very moment, flowing through the universe—through us, through our enemies, our family, our coworkers, and seven billion–plus strangers. There is no limit to it, and it cannot be bottled or protected. It exists everywhere—freely, abundantly, constantly.

Let us be transformed by this knowledge: *Love was never absent from our life.*

Love didn't leave us. It didn't go anywhere. It was never less present for us to access or experience. It was and continues to be ever present, all around us.

We simply allowed our awareness of it to diminish.

The only question now is how well we will serve our destiny in opening up to love and giving it permission to flow. How good and pure a vessel can we be for others in holding the space for love? How strong an amplifier can we be for love? How maturely will we use its unifying energy to complete us, lift us, and unite us?

Our ability to serve this destiny is compromised only by the amount of hurt we have attached to the notion of love. We may have been hurt in our childhood, in our adolescence, in our career, in our relationships. People were nasty. They took advantage of us. They were selfish and broke our trust and hurt our heart. But we must remind ourselves that misfortune had nothing whatsoever to do with love, and if the feelings of sadness, pain, hurt, shame, regret, or heartbreak have darkened the meaning of love, we must now strip away the darkness with the light of truth.

We need not doubt the pain we felt in the past. There was pain.

Yet a loving fate depends on our discovering that
pain has nothing to do with love and that
the time for rekindling past hurts and
living from the motive of fear has run out.

The pain we felt is no longer relevant or cosmically present. If this can be accepted, our understanding of love can be unbound.

As humans capable of vision and choice and will, we must acknowledge that anything of the past is past, that the sour feelings and negativity of yesterday needn't be our choices ever again, that the pain in our past is no longer present unless we choose to make it so.

It must be our intent now, as mature adults, that any pain of the past shall have nothing to do with the reality of love in this moment. Love didn't feel those arrows; *we* did. It is not love's fault, or the fault of the poor souls now receiving our love at half measure, that we chose to pull those arrows from our heart and fling them at our conception of love.

THE ROUTE FROM SUFFERING

The only way through the pain and hurt is love. The surest route from suffering always begins at the trailhead of love.

Let us realize that the walls of protection that we constructed were needless—they protected nothing but perhaps our own bruised egos, since love itself was never capable of being corralled. Even had that been possible, our high barricades may have kept out the villainous, but only at the expense of also keeping out the angels and lovers. All we have done is block love from flowing freely and abundantly in and out of our lives. It is in our self-protection that we often block the very thing we desire.

Once more—it is worth repeating—our diminished concept of love has nothing to do with the real thing. Love remains divine, ever present, all around us, abundant, flowing, accessible now as ever. It is incapable of diminishment except in our own mind.

There was never a time when love was not there for the giving and taking. And there will never be a moment when love has any more potential to heal and nurture than in this moment. So do not fear that one day it will be gone. Love does not ebb in strength over time. It was always and will always be the ever-present unifying force shaping the universe and humankind.

To open up to love once more, we must act on this knowledge—*It was I who diminished love*—and let go of the notion that others must right their past wrongs. We must stop rekindling or resenting ancient hurts. There can be no discovery of fire or treasure there. We have no injuries to avenge now. Let us bind up the wounds of yesterday and set them in the ocean of love. Let no false mental constructs remain about how our love was diminished or broken. Let us finally recast love not as something we "have" but as something that exists independently and abundantly in the world, regardless of our own inadequacies or others' selfishness.

THE BREAKTHROUGH

All breakthroughs in life are merely letting through higher energy—in most cases, that of love. When we tear down the walls of worry and hurt, the bright beams of love may once more shine in and through us. It often only takes a small ray of love from another to burn a permanent hole in the armor of sadness and negativity around our heart.

Released from our confines, no longer hunched in pain, we can stand erect with open eyes, free to sense once more the divine, loving energy in others, no matter how buried they may be by their own fear or hurt. With this recognition, life lights up once more, the full color spectrum returns to our emotional sky, and from within burns a divine fire to care again, connect again, *live* again. We can look past the faults of our brothers and sisters and love them. We can have compassion for an impatient spouse. We can find understanding for a struggling coworker. We can love all humanity once more.

The hardened cynic will predictably cast aside this talk of love's rebirth and redirection. And as long as he does, he will keep himself forever weak, puny, and incapable of any real power or contribution. For as he casts aside love, he loses the ultimate tool for personal transcendence, social good, and influence. Only misery comes to those who criticize the power of love, for they shall be soon cast aside themselves as unwanted and irrelevant, blind and brutish relics of a time gone by in which humanity was trapped in its own fear.

With love resonating through our souls, we are capable of energizing and enlivening those around us with startling power. This energy makes us beautiful to all, even to those who are so concerned with themselves that they can barely see what is right in front of them. This energy gives us access to every power that humans have to create connection with one another: caring, patience, thoughtfulness, kindness, compassion, empathy. It also gives us the charge to lead, activating within us the one virtue needed to unify humankind: courage of the heart.

RISING TO A HIGHER PLANE

When and how will we give ourselves permission to fully love others and ourselves? *Immediately and without condition.*

Does this mean we must *trust* others instantly? No. To transmit love to another, trust is not required. We can love a criminal or miscreant. We need not *trust* them, but as fellow humans and children of God, we can recognize their divinity even though they are not choosing to sense or express it, even if they are attempting to corrupt the incorruptible. All beings come from love, have love in them, and will return to love, even if they are unaware or cruel in their behavior. Avoidance of this truth only permits indifference and hatred to arise.

Surely, trust is needed in relationships. Someone must win our commitment to intimate or romantic love. But to deserve a loving energy from us, one needn't do a thing. Love is not "deserved" by anyone or reserved for only a few. The divine hand gives freely to all.

Must we then accept and respect *the choices and behaviors* of all? No. We can seek to reject, reform, and even punish others for their wrongs. Yet while we do so, we can still intend Love for them, for we needn't lessen ourselves or compromise our role as loving beings just because we must deal with bad behavior. We can punish a selfish and callous child without becoming selfish or callous. We can help a prisoner gain basic human rights and find a love within even if we do not condone his behavior. We can forgive those who trespass against us without giving them our power.

*What this means is that we can have
a divine intent for everyone we meet,
whether or not they deserve it, have asked for it,
or will reciprocate it.*

There can be an emanating love that comes from us regardless of another's intent or behavior. We can release a magnificent spiritual power through our eyes and gestures toward everyone, while expecting no return whatsoever. We can unleash our love into the world for no other reason than because it is our nature to do so.

Love, like any virtue, must be a conscious affair, willed forth, chosen from among all the angelic and wretched impulses available at any moment in the human condition. And so to ascend to greatness and become generous with love, we must be aware of our own weakness and propensity for evil. By never forgetting that we can teeter into darkness, we can remember to look for the light. By remembering the dangers of cruelty, we must will ourselves to be compassionate and loving.

*We are not angels; we are humans.
But let us nonetheless try to rise to a higher plane.*

To sense and amplify love, we do not need to love ourselves—though let that be our goal as well. This popular fantasy that we must first love ourselves before loving others serves no one, for it merely gives us permission to await a good day to love others. Should love be kept from anyone simply because we have insecurities? To give love, we must

only allow it to flow through us, not attempt to own it or sense some false completeness or personal perfection before exuding it. *Love is perfect; we do not need to be.* It is selfish and silly to believe we must love every aspect of who we are to appreciate and adore any aspect of someone else. Surely, it should be our aim to accept and love ourselves, but we can equally disdain any of our peculiar attitudes or behaviors that steal from our freedom, happiness, and connection with others. If we don't like something about ourselves, we can change it, but we needn't await its repair before we fix that great light of love onto others. We shall not wait for the splendid, mythical bright day when we are perfect and always bursting with happiness before allowing our own ray of divinity to shine through to others.

A DIVINE INTENT

To open oneself to and release love is the highest act of courage and the highest freedom. Few among us will have such divine intent or be so brave on a consistent basis. But ours must be a different destiny from that of the bitter, weak, or inattentive. If we wish to be a person of greatness, it will require a stunning release of love into the world.

Let us choose to live a life defined by love. Let us meet the eyes of all and send this message through our thoughts and deeds:

I wish nothing but joy and love for you.

But let us also remember that love, on the human realm, is more than an intention to send others. If there is no actual *demonstration* of active caring and regard for or from another, then we cannot give or sense human love—divine love, surely, as it is all around, but love for or from another must be sensed through *action*, not intent. Thinking is not love—giving is.

Today, like all days of our lives, we have choices to make about what kinds of persons we'll be and how we'll interact with the world. We can meet others with no intention or care. Or we can meet them with disregard and bitterness. Or we can meet them with a profoundly loving intent and fire, a full and vibrant energy that reminds them once more of the spectacular abundance of love and divinity in this world. Which choice we make will determine the quality of our lives, the depth of our relationships, and the hope of our human family.

Declaration VIII

WE SHALL
INSPIRE GREATNESS

I don't know what your destiny will be, but one thing I know:
the only ones among you who will be really happy are those
who will have sought and found how to serve.

ALBERT SCHWEITZER

WHEN A PEOPLE BEGIN TO PERISH FOR APATHY, indifference, or a lack of vision, a voice of leadership must arise. From the squalor of a contaminated moral environment must surface an honorable few unafraid to challenge mediocrity and change the direction of the world. Let us be among those brave few.

As so many choose lives of indolence, let us be unafraid of the demands of greatness and choose to pick up the dimming golden torch of human excellence and ignite it once more with life and power for all to see.

Each of us serves as a living example to others. Our character and conduct can cast either the bright glow of greatness and service to the far corners of our influence, or a shadow of smallness and selfishness to the unfortunate few nearest us. Our striving for a better life and a better world can leave others inspired if it comes from a genuine place of service, or diminished if it comes from a place of greed.

We must have the courage to ask, "In this confused era, am I seeking to be a role model on a daily basis for all of those I love and serve? Am I lifting up those around me? Am I in some way elevating humanity by leading others to see and activate their potential? *Am I living a truly great life?*"

Seeking greatness—*and doing the work to deserve it*—must come back into our collective consciousness. Let us now awaken that powerful force within that seeks to lift some of the weight of the world from the backs of those struggling. Let us take our position as generals of generosity, as leaders of the highest caliber who give a damn about others and the world. Let us declare with firm intent, to the world and ourselves: *We Shall Inspire Greatness.*

A TROUBLED WORLD

The world's people are in peril. We no doubt live in a noisy, numb, narcissistic age. The talents and attentions of the majority are not invested in personal mastery and social responsibility but squandered on games, voyeurism, and base sensationalism. We have recklessly abandoned what truly matters—the striving to be great as individuals and as a society—for the glamour and thrill of speed, convenience, and vain expression, in a kind of humanity-wide midlife crisis. Gone are the big visions; here are the quick wins and the sure things. Effort has lost out to entitlement. In the transition to our age of self-adoration and conceit, the page turned long ago on the dreams to rise as a people. Greatness is so rarely sought, and generation after generation fail to hold the line of human goodness and advancement. *Why?*

Because most people don't want to hold themselves or others to a higher standard, because the former requires discipline and the latter invites conflict. And so they excuse their poor behavior and don't call out social wrongs. They no longer firmly expect themselves or others to act with virtue, compassion, excellence, or wisdom. They look away when their bosses do something wrong. They don't tell their children to improve their behavior because they don't want to be too controlling. They can't tell the team to shape up because they don't want to appear bossy.

Without more people deciding to serve
as role models and leaders, our society has become a suffering case
of the silent and bland leading the silent and bland.

There is a confused complacency—everyone knows there is more for us, but it's just too much trouble to organize ourselves to chase it. It is easier to indulge in our comforts, our profits, our easygoing ways. Such habits have reduced our individual greatness and led to a worldwide failure in leadership. This is evident when we see an apathetic populace, unjustifiable poverty, unconscionable greed, and a world ravaged and booby-trapped by war. If we continue on this path, history will not be kind to us, and a cheated destiny will exact its revenge.

Is there not a person among us who does not think that we can do better if we tried? The naysayers will tell us nothing can be done. They say that the world is going to hell; it is unrecoverable. They imagine that humankind is simply too sad and selfish to be able to right its wrongs. But is this true?

Perhaps some people are indeed so buried in their life's challenges that they can hardly inspire themselves, let alone inspire others. But it is also true that there are some people who are doing their damnedest to improve the world. These people wake each day and fight hard to have a better tomorrow, actively seek learning and challenge in order to grow and contribute, and deeply care about their integrity and the character of their children and communities. If the majority of the world's populace didn't work hard, care for one another, or carry the bright flame of goodness within their souls, then this earth would have perished long ago. Having mastered the atom and the machinery of death that is modern warfare, the mere fact that we are alive now reveals a vast preference toward life and virtue.

And now we are at a fascinating place where billions of us so desperately want the world to improve, and we want something to give to, to believe in, to fight for. We are looking forward to contributing our creativity and sweat and fire to something that matters, to something that improves our lives and the lives of others. We are now tired of waiting. So let us lead.

RIGHTING OUR SHIP

We must begin at home. Let us sit down tonight with our families and take an unflinching look at whom we have become. Are we being solid lovers and parents, good and true children, faithful supporters of those we care for? Is our own house in order? What could we be doing better in the world as a family?

Good people often fail to become great people because they avoid looking honestly at personal lives. They try to lead others but do not lead themselves, and at some point that incongruence catches up with and derails them. So let us ask, "What must I finally face and fix in my own life? Do I need to eat healthier? Then let me do it. Do I need to treat my kids with greater patience and kindness? Then let me begin. Are there tasks I have been putting off that could help my family? Then let me complete them." In addressing our own lives, we ready our minds and spirit to address the world.

As we seek more influence and attempt to change the world, we will draw more attention to our lives. This should inspire us to care about being a role model and motivate us to right our lives. If we are to be solid for our collaborators, let us be solid for our families. If we want people to have energy for their tasks and duties, then let us take care of ourselves so that we are their inspiration. There is no great philosopher or leader who has not taken care to remind us that we must be the change we seek in the world.

STANDING APART

Once we get our homes in order, we must seek to reconnect with the world. Our aim must be to help others find their own meaningful projects and causes. This is a vital distinction in an age when so many leaders are shoving their own agendas down the throats of their people. They have forgotten that service is not a selfish act.

Should we succeed at becoming great, we will need to be very different than the egoists and extremists who have stolen the mantle of leadership and infiltrated the world's psyche.

Look at how sad so many of our so-called leaders have become. They fear becoming unpopular, so they do not make tough or expedient choices, preferring instead endless talk, constant compromise, and obedience to party lines versus public needs. While they are fearful, we shall stand out by being brave.

They are dismissive of those who do not have equal or higher power than themselves, rarely speaking with common people and those on the front lines. While they are elitists, we shall be humble and in the field with those we lead.

They avoid passionate debate and any demonstrations of emotion, hoping to appear always buttoned up, logical. Their humanity becomes that of a computer, dispassionate and disconnected from the heart. While they have abandoned feeling, we shall live with fire and draw in the world so desperate for authentic emotion and connection.

They appear tired, much older than their age, unable to maintain buoyancy in their voice and carriage, long faces and distant gazes betraying exhaustion. While they lack vibrancy, we shall exude it.

Their public discourse and policies cater to the loudest-complaining derelicts and extremists around them, perpetuating language and beliefs that are of the lowest-common denominator while separating us into camps of stupid stereotypes. While they bow to the extremists and communicate with low intelligence, we will bring a third perspective that is collaborative and conscious.

They tend to be reactionary fools, bending and breaking at the whims of a shallow media, and so they stand for nothing and seek to be compliant with the lowbrow nature of mass communication. While they lack dignity and integrity, we shall maintain ours.

They shirk responsibility, always pointing and blaming like spoiled children. While they have remained unaccountable and refused to own their actions and results, we shall always own ours.

They are greedy for the spotlight and the money, and so they stump for more dollars and power. While they are greedy, we shall be simple and fight for those who suffer from lack.

They favor the experts and the comforts of the status quo, forgetting to listen to the youthful and inexperienced who might view the world and its problems from a fresh vantage point. While they dismiss the uninitiated, we shall make them our friends and advisors.

They are cynical, believing that change can come only slowly or through formality and tradition. While they have not experienced the power of a movement, we shall begin a movement of our own.

We must demand these things of ourselves. Let us be so bold as to lead in new ways, standing apart from those who have been failing to raise our businesses, communities, and nations to higher levels of excellence and greatness.

No matter the position we hold
at work, at school, or in our community,
we shall show the world an alternative example
by always caring enough to be remarkable and unifying.

In a world struggling for hope and wanting for light and leadership, we shall seek to shine as beacons.

Few argue that the world is in need of new and different leaders. So let us sit down tonight and write our manifestos for how we will be different. Let us write and write some more: What beliefs and causes will we support? How will we approach the issues and problems of the world in new ways? What will inspire a new movement? How can we rise?

DEMAND HIGHER STANDARDS

If we will make our difference, it will not be alone. And so we must learn soon not to fear demanding that others rise to higher standards should they wish to march with us. If we are to inspire real change and progress, then we must expect more from those around us than others do.

This is not new territory. There is a well-blazed trail to greatness from a long line of hardworking and honorable men and women who gave us the freedoms we enjoy today. What were their secrets to success in achieving great things and inspiring others to contribute? *They were unfailing in their demands for action and excellence.*

Similarly, much of the impact of our legacy in this world hinges on our willingness to demand more from people. *Demand* does not mean to be pushy or commanding, though a leader should not shrink from this. *Demand* means setting expectations, communicating with candor, constantly holding people to high standards by incentivizing those who rise to the challenge while simultaneously calling out and coaching those who do not.

Because many do not like the concept of reprimanding others in today's overly tolerant environment where people want to be friends not leaders, we must revisit the concept.

A society that lacks good people willing to speak against evil or low standards can only devolve into darkness and mediocrity.

When people do something wrong, they need to be told they are doing something wrong. If not, standards slump. The teenager who is hurting others needs to be told to stop, without apology, lest we desire an entire generation of selfish and cruel adults. The politician who is lying needs to be called out lest we desire a nation led by liars. The coworker who cuts corners needs a talking to lest we desire a workplace full of cheaters and schemers. *This is what a virtuous world requires: candid people willing to hold high standards for themselves and others.*

We must learn to shape and confront others' beliefs and behaviors so that everyone is moving forward to a meaningful goal. This often means telling people that they are not measuring up or that they could be contributing in better ways. While terrifying for many—and unpopular in a world that tells its people not to rock any boats or expect anything significant from others—what is the alternative? To keep quiet as the world becomes increasingly apathetic and dishonest and debased?

Some people will tell us not to expect much from others. They will tell us it is unfair to desire more from people. Those who doubt the power and potential of people say, "Go easy on others. They are weak and weary, so set small goals for them or they will feel overwhelmed and, too often, disappointed." These are the catcalls of mediocrity. We must not listen to doubters or allow our small imaginations to cast others as less vital and powerful than their potential, no matter their current state. Who are we to question someone's ability to grow or be great, or to diminish the latent powers of God's children? Let us note the challenges people face, but let us always hold them in high regard and respect. From this place alone we will gain their favor and willingness to rise.

THE NINE VIRTUES OF GREATNESS

What exactly shall we demand of others? The same we demand of ourselves: conduct becoming of a noble character, attention to both our shortcomings and our strengths, a ready willingness to be excellent in our service to the world even when it becomes tiresome and difficult.

We will do this by inspiring and challenging others to act with wisdom and virtue in any part of their lives upon which we have influence. If we have their ear, let us sow the seeds of greatness by inspiring the nine virtues of greatness.

Let us demand honesty. All people want to live proud, upright lives of integrity. They want to be truthful. They hate having to lie, being exposed as liars, and getting caught in the web of others' falsehoods. Yet how easily do these same people make small false claims, and get away with it by an indifferent society? Let us be the ones to hold the line of honesty and call out wherever it is breached. Let us be the ones to push people to be straightforward in their lives. If someone lies, let us speak to them immediately, saying, "I am concerned about your level of honesty." This is called candor, and it demonstrates a willingness to hold people to high standards. We must be uncompromising regarding truth and we must inspire others to be the same.

Let us demand responsibility. Many people have an innate sense of responsibility for their actions, but too many avoid it in the name of ease. They know they should finish the report they promised, but they would rather go to the game. They know it is wrong to not pay their child support, but they prefer to keep the money for their own rent. They know they should be responsible for their actions, but it's easier to duck their duty and blame their parents or culture for their bad behavior. But when someone favors ease over duty, many suffer.

Our job as leaders is to activate and encourage a more responsible nature in those we encounter. When those we influence fail to do their duty or to own their reality, we must help them see the full canvas of negative consequences they are creating for themselves and others. We shall say, "Do you realize that when you failed to complete your responsibility and turn in that report, your entire team was put on hold and left uninformed at the last meeting? Are you aware of the fact that by you not paying child support, your son has taken to stealing food from the corner grocer? Can you see that all this blaming of your parents and culture isn't getting you anywhere, that you alone are responsible for your actions and direction in life regardless of the past?"

It is difficult to point out the mistakes or failings of others, but we must do this if we seek to lead. We can be kind and understanding, but let us be direct and passionate in helping them improve for the future. If we are unwilling to point out when someone is being irresponsible in their duties and behavior, then we are unfit to lead.

Let us demand intelligence. The world has grown full of people ignorant of the grave matters affecting their lives and communities, and only superficially informed in their areas of expertise. Yet as people become more ignorant, they become more cynical—they have not taken the trouble to learn what is true, so they reject the facts that they were too lazy or biased to examine.

We must not continue celebrating ignorance in our society. Our modern culture adores the moron on television, the brainless face in the magazine, the thoughtless extremist on the airwaves. We mustn't be blind to the fact that our children are seeing this and becoming blind themselves. If we are to be great, we must take responsibility to help others learn, explore, think critically, and grow in wisdom.

For all those we influence and lead, we must be role models and expect more thoughtfulness and intelligence. Let us not fail to ask our children to study more, our coworkers to do more research, our media to present more balanced and informed news. If someone asks us an ignorant question, we must encourage them to spend more time preparing. If a coworker acts ignorantly, we must advise them to become more knowledgeable and assign them a mentor. And should we witness true wisdom, genius, or creativity in any area in which we serve, let us be its ultimate champion and incentivize brilliance.

Let us demand excellence. For those destined for greatness, all things must be done well and to completion. We must strive for the highest levels of work and achievement in all we do. And no one within our sphere should be allowed to approach their work with half interest or occasional effort. Should we find such a person in our midst, let us be candid with them about our higher expectation and do all that we are able to help them meet it. But should they fail to meet it swiftly, we should send them as swiftly away. We have no time for mediocrity on our march. Those who do not share our interest in excellence must be left behind, as they will not contribute meaningfully and they cannot be led on our particular path. We have no need to worry about cutting poor performers loose: they will quickly be picked up and find their own place. This is not being dismissive or cruel or unappreciative; it is simply allowing people to find out where their level of contribution and talent is really needed. We do not judge them and we need not seek to "fix" them. On our own journey, we are merely choosing to surround ourselves with those who align with our values and our mission. We must never be shy in setting the expectation for world-class performance. Widely shared, it becomes an unwavering standard that inspires everyone to a higher quality of action.

Let us demand courage. The world's fate lies with the number of its people dedicated to courageous action. In all areas of influence, we must defeat our own fears and instill the same strength into those we care for and serve. We must motivate people not to talk but to act, never allowing others to let words substitute for actual effort. We can help others favor action by asking, "What have you done about it?" as much as we ask, "What do you think about it?"

When we see others shrink in silence or back off from their dreams, we should ask *why.* If their response grows thick with excuse and weakness, we should take it upon ourselves to remind them of their innate powers of will and strength. Courage is often cultivated through confrontation: forcing others to face fears and injustices, teaching people to help rather than hide, asking for candor over quietness, urging others to stand up rather than back down.

Let us demand respect for others. The glow of respect nurtures all other virtues of human connection: kindness, compassion, fairness, empathy, love. We must show *tremendou*s respect to those we seek to inspire, even if we are being strong and demanding with them. And we must ask them to give others the same respect. The more people we lead, the more we can anticipate that there will be disrespect in our ranks, whether toward us or toward others. We shall be kind to the perpetrator yet uncompromising in asking for apology and redress. Give the disrespectful person affection and patience but also clear warning. Do not tolerate any behavior that is dismissive, cruel, or condescending. Should we fail in this, then we ourselves become unworthy of respect.

Let us demand vigilance. Among the great, there is a healthy paranoia, a heightened concern of the dark shadows of apathy that could, at any moment, overtake a shining cause. All that makes consistent success possible—drive, discipline, persistence, commitment—come from a vigilant awareness of what we are fighting for, of what might make us fail, of our ethics, of how successfully we are progressing. We ask for vigilance by focusing everyone's attention on the things that matter and by being honest about progress toward those things. We must constantly say, "Pay attention. Know what we're doing, know where we must do better, and know what stands in our way." Great leaders are on edge in a conscious way—they are alert yet calm.

Let us demand service. Too many have forgotten the charge that our ancestors left us: to direct our energy, knowledge, and talent toward making a difference. What are we all fighting for if not to improve one another's lives? For our families, communities, and world, we must rise in service once more. Service is the intent to do good and do well for others, to be of genuine, warm assistance in their time of need. Do the people around us care deeply for others? Do they want to help people? Do they worry about getting it right and wowing those we strive with and serve?

Those without this virtue in their hearts must not be within our circle. Remove them at once, as the selfish and unconcerned will rip us from glory.

Let us demand unity. The pillars of a community cannot be strong when corroded with gossip and pettiness. We must inspire in others their natural tendencies for tolerance, bonding, and community. We must always remind others, "We are in this together." This is the most basic expectation of all leadership once the proper people are involved: that we are on a march together toward something important; that we must work together, stay together, struggle together, and achieve together.

We must never be the weak, small leaders who start fights within our ranks. Our communication must always carry the theme of togetherness. Do not gossip. Do not divide the team. Do not make one division seem more important than the others.

Should we witness others becoming selfish or demonstrating narrow interests, we shall remind them of their greater connection and service to others. We can praise an individual yet still draw her attention to her positive impact on the team and culture. The moment we succeed is when our people say "us" or "we" more than "I" or "me," when we see our people celebrating wins together, dining together, crying together, striving together.

Honesty. Responsibility. Intelligence. Excellence. Courage. Respect. Vigilance. Service. Unity. These are the virtues of greatness that we must exemplify and expect. These are the virtues that forge remarkable people and may be wielded like a sword against many of the world's ills.

The demands of such virtues are stark and difficult. Some people will question how we can simply leave behind those who fail to meet such high standards. But let's stop the grand delusion that says everyone has to be on every journey we take. The reality is some people won't want to join our march, and they should be allowed to excuse themselves without shame or regret. Not everyone needs to be a part of every initiative and not everyone can live up to the standards of excellence we need in order to achieve the remarkable. And so let's find those who are truly committed and capable and leave the rest to find their own passions and pursuits.

THE DEATH OF DARKNESS

If we inspire ourselves, and those we strive with and serve, to such greatness, what will be its end? Nothing less than the death of mediocrity in our circle of influence. Perhaps it is true that there will always be low standards in an immense society, and perhaps because worldwide change takes so long, only the dead see the end of war and poverty and all other dark social failings. But we the living must nonetheless try. Let us at least strive toward ending many of society's ills. For if we do not, then who will—and when? What will history say if we do not do better?

Can there be a new dawn of humankind in which more of us become great men and women of character and conscience? If we doubt it, we are doomed to fail. But if we lift this mantle from previous generations, carry it further, and share both its burden and its splendor more widely, then we shall become examples of greatness that the children of the future shall celebrate and aspire to. Let us, then, out of respect for the blood and hard-won triumphs of those who have inspired us, and in duty to those who we love and serve and those we shall never know who await inspiration, *arise now* and *become great.*

Declaration IX

WE SHALL SLOW TIME

The aim of life is to live, and to live means to be aware,
joyously, drunkenly, serenely, divinely aware.

HENRY MILLER

IFE IS MEANT TO BE A VIBRANT, DEEPLY FELT, growing mosaic of meaningful moments. It is to be a grand, fully engaged, and unconditionally committed love affair with our daily experience. We are supposed to feel this and sense this, to engage with whatever appears in front of us with awareness and enthusiasm, joyfully unwrapping the gifts that fate has chosen to bring.

We are not supposed to miss this moment. We were not destined to go barreling through life half-numb, unaware of our senses and surroundings, deaf and blind to the magical qualities of the moment. This day is to be enjoyed like a pause at a cool stream during summer's heat. Even in darker times, we should look around us with awe, taking in the beautiful scenes and small wonders that surely abound, fascinated even with any hint of hope in the darkness, like staring into a moonlit field alive with a million silent fireflies.

We are not supposed to miss this moment. Our brain was not built for this frenzy, forced to focus on everything yet nothing, sped up and buzzed out by syrups and stimulants, crammed with so much random negative information and so many pointless tasks that there is never a singular focal point to immerse in or achieve or celebrate.

We are not supposed to miss this moment. Our bodies were not designed for the atrophy of a sedentary life choked full of laziness and sloth and hours sitting behind desks, robbed of the pleasures of touch and movement and the blessed physical exhaustion from a good day's work actually doing something or building something.

We are not supposed to miss this moment. Our soul was not meant to be trapped in the past, weighted by futile attachments to longstanding stories, caged by old angers and regrets, unable to sense and soar in the white and clean emotional expanse of Now.

We are not supposed to miss this moment. Our families do not desire a life of frenzied urgency; they do not want our absence, in mind or body, to be their only memory of us.

We are not supposed to miss this, this *life*. But we do, all frazzled, stressed, and stripped away from the moment. The cost is immense—so many moments blurred by speed and worry and panic, creating the catastrophe of a joyless life.

We can experience so much more of life. It takes very little focus and effort to increase our awareness of the gift of each day, to insert more depth and feeling and meaning in life again. Let us make that our aim. We must shift our focus away from the chaos and back to the true order of the universe, which gives us unrestricted freedom and peace in this moment. We must breathe once more. We must drink in our surroundings and let our bodies feel again. We must connect our heart to our life, putting hope and passion and love back into the efforts of the hour. This requires only a new deployment of our attention, time, and energy, a different intention and pace to life. We must slow it all down so that we can feel it once more, enjoy it once more, *live* it perhaps for the first time. This is the moment to finally begin to enjoy life's blessings. Let us declare: *We Shall Slow Time*.

TIME IS FINITE

This is the predictable cry of the bewildered and regretful: *I thought there would be more time.*

We say it when our children leave home, as if we had planned one day, someday in the future when we were less stressed, to appreciate and admire them before they took wing. *I thought there would be more time to enjoy them and watch them grow.*

We say it when our job is yanked from us, as if acknowledging that we had more to give, as if it were unfair that we didn't get to give it, as if we were waiting one day to show up and perform and contribute for real. *I thought there would be more time to demonstrate excellence and make my mark.*

We say it when our lover leaves, catching us off guard, as if we were blindsided, given no indication, as if it were not our fault that the magic had left long before, as if someday we were going to be a better partner. *I thought there would be more time to express how much I love you.*

We say it as we die, as our last, failing grip on reality is being released by a bigger Hand, the air slipping from our lungs, the pain fading from intense to an odd dullness and finally to peace and light. Should we have lived an unfelt and regretful life, we would say this to ourselves, as if we were always planning to live someday soon, as if caught by surprise that there is at last no more time to live and love and matter, as if we hadn't realized the clock was ticking all along, as if we hadn't known we would be called. *I thought there would be more . . .*

Did we not know all this? How do we so foolhardily miss the irony of it all? That here in an infinite universe, time is finite for us, that even if we cannot discern the order and reason for it all, the outcome is predictable—life will randomly, and too soon, be taken away, perhaps brutishly or easily, but likely with little fanfare or crescendo other than, hopefully, the love that has gathered around us.

Why, when that moment arrives, do so many gasp and beg and plead for one more hand of cards, as though the Dealer would keep patience for a drifter who never even fully played the cards He had already so generously dealt?

We could bemoan the coming decline. We could seek to avert the day death arrives and whispers in our ear that now is our destined moment to ascend back to Love. We could deny that it will happen. We could keep missing all the hints we receive to enjoy life while we can, as people we love die, accidents happen, randomness strikes like lightning from a clear sky. But instead, we don't think about our mortality either way. We continue checking our fancy watches and full agendas in a panic, wondering where we are to be, somehow blind and deaf to destiny waving its arms, crying out in this very moment of reality, saying, *My friend, my friend, you are where you are supposed to be already, do you not see? Stop looking for something else and look and feel all around. Everything is here now. Miss it, and you will have missed life.*

NOTHING BUT NEWNESS

Too many have fled this moment for yesterday or tomorrow, dreaming of a time and place they would rather be. To what result? Those who are alive but who are in a sense living in a different time from now are ghosts. They are never fully seen or sensed by their loved ones; the bounty of the universe cannot find them to gift them; they are dissipated, absent from the roll call of Now.

Let us not continue making this mistake of being so absent from our day, from this moment. We do not need to feel ashamed that we have been absent, and we must not be bitter to those who have been absent from us. We have missed moments, but that cannot be undone. Our lack of presence yesterday with those we love and lead is done—those moments shall not return, no matter how we hope to rope them in with heartache. What we missed, we missed. Do not now add the weight of sadness.

We can add nothing to yesterday, and we should attach nothing to what we did or did not do, for all those moments are in the ether now, stranded only in the stories in our minds.

Nor should we harbor any bitterness toward others, because over time, our sense of disconnection likely equaled theirs, and in condemning them we condemn ourselves. Some people didn't see us needing them. Some didn't care. It does not matter now.

All that matters is what is here now before us, to be lived and defined and experienced as we choose.

We can breathe deeply today and notice that there is no scent of yesterday. In this moment, there is nothing but newness, a white space, nothing but an open field of possibility ready to be felt and explored. Let us meet it with an intention and skill in exploring it lovingly, *slowly*.

THE SENSORY ANIMAL

To slow down the moment, we must heighten our senses. To feel something more, we must either take more in, or more deeply sense that which is already here.

We all have vivid memories of times when a crisis or beautiful moment seemed to slow down time. We rounded a corner and saw an accident; we sat by the side of someone we loved as they died; we watched proudly in the audience as our children graduated. In these moments, our heightened alertness made the scene unfold in slow motion. With knowledge of this power, we can choose to direct it at will, to slow down our experience of time and of life itself.

It is in our nature to sense our environment. We are highly attuned sensory animals. Our gifts of vision, smell, touch, taste, and hearing can be aimed and used like a great receiver to pull in and magnify this moment's streaming current.

Slowing time begins, always, with the *breath*. The deeper and longer we draw air in, the more oxygenated our bodies become, and the more heightened our energy and presence. Yet most of us are not aware of how we breathe. We are shallow breathers, dumbly sipping from this deep, refreshing pool of oxygen around us. On the rare instances when we use our breath, it comes in huffs and grunts of displeasure or exertion. But life can never be fully felt if we are not breathing in the moment and oxygenating our brains to full power and alertness through deep and present breathing. When we attune to our breath and deepen and lengthen the volume of air that we draw in, it has an immediate and extraordinary impact on how we experience the moment. Before we give a speech or performance, we can breathe. Before a tough conversation with a lover or friend, we can breathe. When we are waiting in line at the store, working out, or sitting at our desks, we can remember to take in life and feel it through every breath.

Let us try to bring our awareness to our breath now. We should draw air into our bellies as if filling a great balloon, feeling the air all the way up into our chest, then let it out smoothly, with controlled ease. It is difficult, if not impossible, to do this type of breathing every moment— our subconscious will quickly take the helm back and resume shallow breathing. But it can be conditioned to last longer; if we focus on it, the practice becomes stronger and, over time, more automatic. To be more present, let us check into our breath several times in the hour and especially in moments that we want to feel and remember.

We can further slow time by absorbing more details from our surroundings. We should take note of the color, texture, and placement of objects around us. We can notice the way the tree branch sways rhythmically with the wind as we gaze out the window. We can observe the smooth and perfect skin of a baby, touching her soft cheek and mimicking her expressions. We can watch the cloud formations as they make lazy shapes in the sky. We can see how artfully food is arranged on a plate, with the vibrant greens and oranges of each ingredient. This effort is not a race. *Scanning our surroundings like beasts on the run is not what we are after.* Our aim is to drink in the moment, and so we should pause and truly see what is in front of us.

It is the curious and unhurried eye
that brings color back to life.

Slowing time continues by heightening our awareness of touch—our physical sensation of the moment. We should touch more things around us, pick up things and turn them in our hands and take in their dimensions, texture, and details. Kissing our lover, we should feel their lips as if this were the most important kiss. When we walk, we should walk in presence, feeling how our heels and toes touch the earth. Our skin holds the keys to a life truly felt, to real pleasures of experience.

And what do we hear now? Too often we tone down the sounds of life. We should love the sounds in our ears: the car driving by; the house finch trilling in the birch tree; the beautiful, unique voice speaking to us. For us to slow and enjoy life, we must enjoy the music of the world around us. This does not mean we cannot tune out the irritable, but there is a difference between tuning some things out and turning off all things.

Finally, no sense in our hasty world is so brutishly ignored as that of taste. Ours is a culture that gulps its food like starving hyenas. We don't often let food linger; we don't delight in its texture and its finish. Many have no memory of their last meal because they barely experienced eating it. We must return to more dignified times, when food was not something we wolfed down on the run, but something with meaning that brought nourishment, joy, and connection into our lives. Let us take real pleasure in what we are eating, and if what we are eating doesn't bring true enjoyment and health to our bodies, then let us push it aside.

It is such a simple formula: The more senses we bring to the moment, the more time slows, the more a catalogue of joyful vivid memories grows in our minds, the more life is filled with gratitude, and the more nourished our soul.

AWARENESS CAN STOP TIME

To those who cannot sense and slow time, we need only remind them of the times it happened almost automatically.

> "Remember when you were immersed in your art and everything narrowed around you?"

> "Remember when you slowed time and breathed in the smell of your lover?"

"Remember when you gave that gift and watched his face as he unwrapped it, and how his smile seemed to happen so quickly at the time, yet the moment lingered so long? And now, as it plays back in your mind, how that smile slowly spreads across his face as if the more days that pass, the longer that smile lingers, even as its brilliance never fades?"

"Remember when the world stopped as you listened closely to your friend sharing her pain and you just felt for her?"

"Remember when you walked into the meadow or the woods or the sand and looked out on the vista of nature, and it felt as if you were a part of it and it a part of you, that magical immensity and power of nature taking your breath away?"

"Remember that plate of food that you relished every single bite of, wishing the meal would never end and the tastes would never fade?"

"Remember the sounds of the concert you waited so long for, that pulsing in your ears that seemed to beat with your own heart?"

It was as if we put time itself on hold so that we could sense something that was timeless, beautiful, meaningful. These needn't be rare moments.

There can be an everyday magic to our experience, and that magic need not be mystical but, rather, a conscious trick of elongating time, of heightening and deepening our senses to the moment.

Awareness is humanity's best weapon against time. So let us always remember our capacities to be gifted time benders. We have an extraordinary ability to slow the moment down, to wade into it, to feel it swirl and surround us. Along with the powers of will and motivation, the ability to fully sense and heighten our experiences helps us combat staleness and live a truly free and vibrant life.

TWO BEATS LONGER

What would happen to the quality of our life and relationships if we simply amplified our senses just a little longer?

Let us forget for now where we are supposed to be and what we should be doing. Instead, let us hold *this* moment for just *two beats longer.*

Do not breathe so quickly. Take in air for two beats longer.

Do not scan the room. *Sense* the room by gazing into each shadow and corner for two beats longer.

Do not merely glance at her. Look into her eyes and hold them for two beats longer.

Do not gulp down the next meal but savor each bite for two beats longer, let the tastes melt and linger.

Do not send the heartless note. Read it once more and spend two beats longer sensing the pain it may cause another.

Do not give a perfunctory kiss good-bye while juggling everything on the way out the door. Make the kiss *count*, make it firm and solid and true, holding the moment passionately for two beats longer.

Life is lived in the extra beats we hold as time unfolds. Soon, the two beats become four, the four become eight, and eventually we will have mastered the art of experiencing life, of feeling who we are and where we are on our path to greatness, of creating real moments, of living as joyous masters in the infinite and divine Freedom of Now.

THE
9 DECLARATIONS

———••———

I.   MEET LIFE WITH FULL PRESENCE AND POWER

II.   RECLAIM YOUR AGENDA

III.   DEFEAT YOUR DEMONS

IV.   ADVANCE WITH ABANDON

V.   PRACTICE JOY AND GRATITUDE

VI.   DO NOT BREAK INTEGRITY

VII.   AMPLIFY LOVE

VIII. INSPIRE GREATNESS

IX.   SLOW TIME

———••———

MEET THE AUTHOR

BRENDON BURCHARD is one of the most widely followed personal development trainers of our time. He is a #1 *New York Times* best-selling author whose books include *Life's Golden Ticket, The Millionaire Messenger,* and *The Charge: Activating the 10 Human Drives that Make You Feel Alive.*

After surviving a car accident at the age of 19, Brendon received what he calls "life's golden ticket": a second chance. Since then, he has dedicated his life to helping others find their charge and share their voice with the world.

Brendon's efforts have inspired hundreds of millions of people around the globe. He is one of the Top 100 Most Followed Public Figures on Facebook; his weekly YouTube show is the most viewed direct-to-camera personal development series in the history of the site; his motivational podcast, *The Charged Life,* debuted at #1 on iTunes across all categories in the United States and multiple countries; and his blog posts rank as many of the most liked and shared in the modern history of the motivational genre. As a popular conference speaker, he has shared the stage with the Dalai Lama, Sir Richard Branson, Katie Couric, Steve Forbes, Arianna Huffington, Wayne Dyer, Tony Robbins, and hundreds of the world's leading thinkers and innovators.

Brendon is also the founder of High Performance Academy, the legendary personal development program for achievers, and Experts Academy, the world's most comprehensive marketing training for authors, speakers, life coaches, and online thought leaders. For these works, Larry King named him "one of the top motivation and marketing trainers in the world."

Recognized as a thought leader in human motivation and business marketing, Brendon is the recipient of the Maharishi Award and sits on the Innovation Board at XPRIZE Foundation.

Meet Brendon, and receive free resources on motivation and high performance, at BrendonBurchard.com.